PRAISE FOR *ZERO TO HERO*

'If you're serious about improving your ~~sales~~ ~~g~~
Serge Nicholls, New Business Director, Ogilvy Group UK

'This book will push your sales team out of their comfort zone and introduce a mindset change that will take their sales performance to a new level. *Zero to Hero* gets straight to the fundamentals of how to effectively maximize your chances of delivering greater sales success and provides a practical, proven system to guide you through the common obstacles encountered along the way. Whatever your level of sales experience, these techniques will deliver results.'
Judy Hill, Corporate Services Director, Robert Horne Group

'A very handy and useful book which is easy to read and full of practical tips of all the different sales scenarios a sales person can be confronted with. A must-have for the real professional.'
Steven Debrabander, Regional Sales Training & Development Manager, DHL Express – Asia Pacific

ZERO
TO
HERO

ZERO
TO
HERO

SEVEN STEPS TO REVOLUTIONIZE YOUR SALES
Greg Anyon

Copyright © 2010 Greg Anyon

First published in 2010 by Marshall Cavendish Business
An imprint of Marshall Cavendish International

5F / 32–38 Saffron Hill
London EC1N 8FH
United Kingdom

and

1 New Industrial Road
Singapore 536196
genrefsales@sg.marshallcavendish.com
www.marshallcavendish.com/genref

Marshall Cavendish is a trademark of Times Publishing Limited

Other Marshall Cavendish offices: Marshall Cavendish International (Asia) Private Limited, 1 New
Industrial Road, Singapore 536196 • Marshall Cavendish Corporation. 99 White Plains Road, Tarrytown
NY 10591–9001, USA • Marshall Cavendish International (Thailand) Co Ltd. 253 Asoke, 12th Floor,
Sukhumvit 21 Road, Klongtoey Nua, Wattana, Bangkok 10110, Thailand • Marshall Cavendish (Malaysia)
Sdn Bhd, Times Subang, Lot 46, Subang Hi-Tech Industrial Park, Batu Tiga, 40000 Shah Alam, Selangor
Darul Ehsan, Malaysia

The right of Greg Anyon to be identified as the author of this work has been
asserted by him in accordance with the Copyright, Designs and Patents Act 1988.

The author and publisher have used their best efforts in preparing this book and disclaim liability arising
directly and indirectly from the use and application of this book. All reasonable efforts have been made to
obtain necessary copyright permissions. Any omissions or errors are unintentional and will, if brought to
the attention of the publisher, be corrected in future printings.

A CIP record for this book is available from the British Library

ISBN 978-0-462-09951-4

Designed and typeset by www.stazikerjones.co.uk

Printed and bound in Great Britain by
TJ International, Padstow, Cornwall

For Geoff Anyon, who could sell sand to the Arabs
and refrigerators to Eskimos

CONTENTS

Introduction   XI

Chapter 1   11
Step 1: What does highly successful selling look like?

Chapter 2   29
Step 2: And THE most important thing in selling is?

Chapter 3   53
Step 3: Who are you going to sell to?

Chapter 4   73
Step 4: How are you going to get the door open?

Chapter 5   109
Step 5: How will you get them to reveal the really juicy stuff?

Chapter 6   141
Step 6: What happens when they say 'Get Lost'?

Chapter 7   159
Step 7: How do you get the buying organization to bite off
your hand for the proposition?

Chapter 8   175
The Powerhouse Support Team!

Summary   199

Conclusion   207
About the Author   212

INTRODUCTION

HEAD SPACE

Do you want to sell more? Do you want to nail your sales targets to the wall? Do you want to kick the legs out from under your competitors, even in the toughest recessionary market conditions? Do you want to strive for **and achieve** as close to the top of your sales game as possible?

If the answer to those questions is 'Yes' you came to the right place. This book clearly identifies the methodology and skills necessary to target and win significant new business **as quickly and effectively as possible**. You're in charge here. You make the decisions about why the business is significant. In sales it's normally because it is high volume but it should be because it is high VALUE. You can also apply this method to your existing major customers to refresh and develop the relationship and what you get from it.

This is not a quickie recipe in a cheap magazine. It's a thumping great cook book equipping you with the recipes, ingredients and cooking instructions to prepare a feast. It also gives you **step-by-step** directions for laying the table, choosing the music, devouring the courses and clearing up afterwards.

THE PURPOSE OF SELLING – THE P WORD

There is an old saying in selling: turnover is vanity, profit is sanity. I understand that there are not-for-profit organizations (who nevertheless are still interested in making lucrative sales), or that we have a production plant to feed and that this month we need volume at the expense of profit. But as a rule of life my genuine belief is that if we cannot create a meaningful profit stream, we just aren't doing it right!

Do you find yourself having to bend your margins over backwards just to limbo under the new-business bar; squeezing those margins in the often futile hope that you will be able to raise the bar later once you have established yourself as a useful and reliable supplier? Look down the road a year or two: entrenched as their main provider, do you still find yourself under margin pressure from your customers? Well, the good news is that the methodology in this book is also designed specifically to help you protect and justify your sales margins from the outset of the sale.

SELLING AS IT SHOULD BE

I like to think that in broad terms there are two types of selling out there in the world today: **traditional** (or **transactional**) and **consultative**. Traditional selling (product or service-based) is what's used by that classic foot-in-the-door sales person who won't take 'No' for an answer. Ask most buying contacts (anyone in a position of purchase authority) these days to describe a traditional sales person and the image isn't a complimentary one: self interested, money-centred, fake and shallow. And these are the nice adjectives. While experience has shown some merit in persistence, very often it angers and irritates. Under these circumstances traditional selling produces heat but not much light. Put another way, it produces nowhere near the actual output that it should.

To define the consultative alternative accurately we need a little expertise, and being an expert is knowing when to call in the experts! So if we go to Wikipedia for a quick definition it describes Consultative Selling (needs-based) like this:

Consultative selling emphasizes customer needs and meeting those needs with solutions combining products and/or services. A consultative salesperson typically provides detailed instruction or advice on which solution best meets these needs. During the prospecting phase of selling, where a customer's needs and wants are examined, the salesperson pays close attention to economical and high-quality solutions for the customer, ideally making sure the prospect receives more value from the product or service they have purchased than they have paid to ensure a positive return on investment (ROI).

As a description of what is now a far from new idea, it is quite thorough. However, the model has moved on. As great as Consultative Selling was, everything must develop if it is to maintain a razor's edge. **Cascade Selling** is today's practical evolution of the old consultative model. It is a non-fluffy, non-academic and not-for-the faint-hearted reinvigoration of everything you ever knew about selling. It trims away the fat, the fluff and the outdated, whilst validating the tried and tested. It takes the hardcore elements, the critical areas of expertise and strips them bare, opening them up to the harshest scrutiny to identify the most expedient method of smashing your sales goals.

Cascade Selling helps sales people reposition themselves for highly successful selling in the following ways:

1. Cascade sales people are as highly evolved, skilled and focused as fighter pilots. They are masters of strategy, tactics, mechanics and movement in pursuit of the perfect mission in a high-speed and highly complex environment. But at the same time they make it look so simple that you would think monkeys could do it.

2. Cascade sales people know that they should not be seen by prospects or customers as **sales people**. Instead they should be seen as **business people**; people with whom a prospect or customer feels reassured to do business (buy from).

3. Even better: that the business person should be seen as a CONSULTANT. But not with all the negative connotations that are evoked by the imagery of someone that tells you the time using your own watch, charging you an arm and a leg to do it! (While of course the consultant actually helps you find and service your watch, and then

shows you how to change the battery so that it keeps good time. But never mind – ooh; touched a nerve there then!)

4. Let's think about the medical consultant. This is a person to whom we go for an expert opinion and advice. We trust them to skilfully assess our symptoms and accurately diagnose the **problem**. Then we trust them to prescribe the best form of treatment.

5. Cascade sales people avoid many of the omnipresent sales behaviours, many of which are hidden, and that *automatically* trigger conflict and failure.

6. They also recognize that Cascade Selling is based on different types of people buying from different types of people – and that in a high percentage of sales, being bright, enthusiastic, happy and friendly far from helping the sale will actually cause it to crash and burn.

7. Cascade Selling causes the sales person to step into the buying contact's moccasins to identify the intrinsic buying catalysts. They will play to as many of the buying turn-ons, and circumnavigate as many of the turn-offs, as possible.

THE 9/11 EFFECT

Prior to the global 'recession' it would probably have been fair to say that in the pursuit of major sales traditional selling no longer had a useful place. With this recession it has become much tougher for many companies to do any kind of business, let alone the lucrative variety. But some industries have been in this position more recently. Immediately following 9/11 (and for some years after), with their survival at stake, I heard it reported from inside the industry that the airlines reverted to a highly transactional method of doing business in order to crush their cost-base. Ostensibly, all supply relationships were severed and electronic bidding or tendering was introduced as the qualification bar under which any supplier had to pass just to get to the point where they could begin serious negotiations for contracts. As you can imagine, sales margins were devoured like a Piranha on a Big Mac, and since then doing business has been extremely unpleasant.

A couple of years ago I heard tell of a services company in the airline industry that was invited to present for a new contract. The supplier was asked to visit the potential customer. As they were ushered into the conference room, the selling team looked around suspiciously for the torture devices upon which they expected to be impaled and bled of their margins. Surprisingly, however, none was to be found. As they were setting up their LCD projector and laptop to do their corporate presentation the buying contacts filed in and stopped them. The lead contact, somewhat unusually, said: 'Please take a seat; *we* will be presenting to *you*.'

He then projected a single PowerPoint slide onto the white screen. It looked very similar to this:

┌──────────── **FanfAir** ──┐
│ Our new supplier will: │
│   │
│ – Work with us to identify key areas of our │
│   business where they can provide │
│   initiatives to help us control, reduce or │
│   eradicate costs. │
│ – Partner us over the longer-term to help us │
│   innovate cost-control strategies and add │
│   value to our business. │
│   │
└─ *We'll Blow You Away...* ──┘

Look at the customers where you are seen as a high-value supplier. Think about the ones with whom you have really productive and seemingly unbreakable relationships.

These things don't happen because you **sell** to them. You don't achieve key supplier status unless you are doing something pretty special, right? If you actually stop the daily carousel spinning and get off for long enough to analyze **why** your successful relationships are successful – the messages in the slide will drop into place like a massive penny. They give us valuable insight into some of the factors in highy successful selling.

Cascade Selling gives us a refined approach. In pursuit of our best interests (yes – we are allowed best interests too) it demands that **we stop selling!** Don't be seen to sell. Don't be thought of by our prospects and customers as self-interested sales people.

Stop selling and start problem solving! The airline had operated the Piranha Policy with their supply chain to find that it was actually not in its own interest to do so. If you strip everything back to the cheapest price, all the value goes too. If you buy 'cheap', the best that you get is basic. The worst that you get is not-fit-for-purpose. Without the value you lose much of what produces the results. If you are ravaging your supplier on a daily basis, the supplier is unlikely to feel good. If they don't *feel* good they won't invest themselves in the relationship. And if they don't do that they also won't go the extra mile. They won't be creative, committed and look after the best interests of the buying business like it was their own.

So the airline decided to be bold and look once again for the missing ingredients. Just as the slide illustrates, the best relationships are formed because the prospect or customer sees us as more than sales robots because:

1. Prior to approaching them we have conducted sufficient research to have formed a working knowledge of their business and the kind of challenges that they face. This buys us credibility and status.
2. We work with them taking a problem-solving approach. We identify key problems in their business.
3. We help them to see the damage that the problems cause. Only then will they recognize a significant need.
4. We provide bespoke solutions to those established and agreed needs. Aha: the 'Selling'!
5. We are seen not as an external supplier but as an essential internal asset in the smooth operation of their business because we become their in-house efficiency consultants.

THE GREAT DETECTIVE

Inside the prospect's or customer's business we need to do a Sherlock Holmes. At the heart of practical Cascade Selling is the very real need to become detectives, and the clues that we seek look like this:

1. Help your prospects and customers identify their present and future problems, and the actual money cost of the problems.

Step into the moccasins of the people that you sell to for a moment. Think about what goes on in their business lives. Think about their daily chores, toils and pressures. Think about their problems. Most prospects and customers are so mind-bendingly **busy** that half of them aren't even conscious of problems. Same-cr*p-different-day is probably how they think of it. And you can't just step in out of the blue, point your finger and start **telling** them what problems they have! Nobody wants to be told they've got a problem especially by a complete stranger. **Especially by a self-interested sales person!** And it's very rare that they would reveal a problem to a sales person anyway, because the information will just get used against them. If you are going to revolutionize your sales results, you've got to get them to want to tell you their problems.

And for this to be as bronze-tanned-sexy as possible you have to think about **big scale** problems. We're talking about big-banner issues on which your products and services can have a significant impact: costs, sales, output, productivity, efficiency, performance and profit. The bigger the problem, the more likely the customer or prospect is to be interested in having it solved. Let's say that their IT system is five years old and designed for 20 users, and there are now 30. A slightly old IT system doesn't sound like much, but as a result it is slower than it could be compared to more modern ones. Productivity is 20 per cent lower than it could be. And the system crashes twice a week for a minimum of an hour, which means that at least 20 users can't work. They're not actually earning their salaries. Additionally, valuable customer order information isn't entered in time to make delivery deadlines. Customers are getting annoyed, and some are already placing orders elsewhere. And some of the sales people who look after them are starting to get disgruntled. A reduction in staff morale doesn't sound like much, but it is.

Help your customer or prospect see the problems that they've got today. What happens if you find a small problem today and do nothing about it? Tomorrow, what does it become? It becomes a **bigger** problem, right? If their IT infrastructure is slow today, it will be crashing tomorrow. If staff morale is low today, people will be leaving tomorrow. So our job is also to help them see that *there may be trouble ahead* and in both cases accurately identify the financial costs.

2. Help them identify their opportunities and the actual money value of them.

There is a view that says: if you help them fix a problem you create an opportunity. Let's say that as an IT consultancy you help your customer fix the problem. And as a result you therefore are instrumental in them recovering £200,000 in productivity, staff and customer retention costs. What can the company then do with that recovered capital? They can either show it as profit or they can invest it. Let's say that they invest it in marketing, which in turn leads to one million pounds in new business. You have the right to *claim credit* for that sum as part of the value that you can provide when you show them how you can solve their problems.

3. Identify the actual money value of you solving the problems, and fulfilling the opportunities.

Imagine yourself as the head of a business, the ultimate decision maker, with the choice of two suppliers. One will work with you deep inside your organization as an essential internal asset identifying, measuring and solving problems in pursuit of the smooth operation of your business. Your in-house efficiency consultants: your business partners. And the other will always say, 'We can do that' and quote you a cheap price for products and services. Which one do you *really* want to buy from? Which choice makes real long-term economic sense?

You have to demonstrate to the customer your physical value as their partner supplier. Many sales people and sales organizations miss a major opportunity every day of the week with this one. They go above and beyond the call of duty on a regular basis in servicing the customer, and expect them to see it, recognize it and value it. Customers have the shortest memory in the world. You have to show them the money. Keep a log of your actions that are not part of the standard service, and calculate the financial gain to the customer for each action. In this way, whenever you have a formal conversation on service level agreements, for example, you have the evidence to justify your position. You also have the greatest piece of negotiating leverage in the world when it comes to negotiations. If they decide that it's time for you to reduce your prices because of a competitive offer, you can rebut it with the (substantial) amount that you are already saving them.

There are a couple of caveats here. First, 'Partner' and 'Partnership' are dangerous words. They get used wholesale by sales people and organizations alike: 'We want to enter into a partnership with our customers...' What this traditionally means is we don't want our customers to give us a rough time and beat us up for better prices.

For years sales organizations have been promoting partnership without delivering it. Partnership is a Nike moment – you can't talk about it. Don't ever say it to prospects or customers because they won't believe it. **Just do it!**

Second, no matter how well we think we have positioned ourselves it is always possible, of course, that you can engage in the above activities, and then they decide to buy it cheaper somewhere else anyway. Often this happens because we are selling to the wrong people in the organization; Purchasing for example. I defy anyone in Purchasing to open their mouths *without* the words 'You're much too expensive...' rushing out. They can't help themselves and have no desire to, which questions the logic of selling value to them, doesn't it? So, more on this later...

Cascade Selling brings refinement and exactness to the sales process – and it is a process. Traditionally it is believed that the most successful transactional sales are not made based on controlled structure but on the *power of personality*: charm, charisma and 'the gift of the gab'. Certainly it's fantastic fun to watch and do, but there are major downsides. 'Power of personality' only ever appeals to a low percentage of prospects so the wastage factor is high, and eventually a wheel will come off and flame-grill a major sales opportunity.

A sale happens either by design or by accident: because of the sales person's skill or because of the buying contact's desire. When a sale fails, in a very high percentage of cases it is because of something that the sales person does, or does not do. There are seven key steps in Cascade Selling that directly govern success or failure. Improving just one of these areas will shorten the sales cycle and accelerate the sale. Become accomplished in all seven areas and an average sales person can become a high-performance hero!

CHAPTER 1

STEP 1
WHAT DOES HIGHLY SUCCESSFUL SELLING LOOK LIKE?

HEADBANGER

There are millions of sales people around the world all selling in a variety of different ways. Some are selling intuitively; doing what feels right based on experience. Others went on a training course at the start of their career and are still following the process they learned. There are others who employ a combination of trained and evolved methodology and skills. Whichever way you do it – it's all good, so long as you are getting worthwhile results and a decent return on your effort, right?

And yet there are still companies out there that, for example, running telesales teams where the telesales person is making hundreds of calls per day. Why are they making this many calls? Well it's not because they're *really outgoing* or are collecting contacts for the Facebook record. It's because they've been targeted to do so. Along the way they are also being rejected hundreds of times per day! I'm not interested in this kind of selling, if for no other reason than it's destructive for the sales person and **it doesn't work anywhere near well enough!**

Can you believe that there are still companies out there for which it is common practice to set numerically high call targets? *Today John, you will make 100 telephone cold calls! Today John you will visit 20 companies!*

Do you know what is wrong with setting this kind of call target? At the end of the day you ask John how many calls he made. You are very pleased when he tells you he called 100 companies! Fabulous – he hit his call target! Then he says to you, beaming with pride: 'I would have called 101 but the last person I called actually asked me what I was selling!'

If you take the view that selling is a numbers game, all you will do is focus on the quantitative input and output. 'We have to make 100 calls to get one face-to-face meeting. 30 per cent of our face-to-face meetings turn into orders with an average value of £1,000. If our financial target is £3,000 we will have to make 1,000 calls to hit it.' What a primitive way of destroying a sales person's will to live and desire to succeed. Why waste all that resource? Why not just have them head-butt the desk until they pass out from blood loss?

NEVER MIND THE QUALITY...

A hypnotic focus on quantity management will produce some sales but it factors **out** the **skill**, which is a tad west of productive. It fails to produce highly successful sales people who consistently deliver the results! You've got to focus on the qualitative stuff **first**.

How do you find out what highly successful selling really looks like? Well, here it is in plain English:

1. Identify what your selling looks like today: the process that you go through (no matter how simple or complex), the tools, skills and techniques that you use. Sketch it out or write it down – draw a map of the steps and stages that you employ from the start of the process to the finish. (There's a map coming up to give you some idea of what one looks like.)
2. Then get a red pen and highlight the areas in your process where you struggle; where you hit objections (perhaps the same ones every time); where you feel like you start losing control of the sale; or where you feel there is definite room for improvement but aren't sure what kind. Or highlight where you just want some fresh ideas or input.
3. If you are going to do this via the self-development route, you will then do some research to identify a well-proven template against which you can compare your own methodology. This means finding a sales model that works for your environment and doing a gap analysis: identify the difference between your model and the template and then build the difference into your new and improved method.

4. There are only a couple of challenges with doing it this way. First, most sales people believe that their market, products and customers are unique so cannot fit a 'standard' model. Second, **finding** a decent model outside of a paid-for sales training course is far from easy!

Let's dig a bit deeper into the comments at point 4 above. I have worked with organizations that employ everything from 3 to 27 stages in their sell. And here's the surprising thing: after refining the process with hundreds of companies it is safe to say that most organizations (including yours) need no more than seven stages to get to the first major commitment in a high value sale (and any other kind for that matter).

BULLSEYE

So, what does a decent sales model that works for your environment look like? The most successful sales happen because they follow a well-proven path, designed to get them from the beginning, through the middle to end in the most **expedient manner possible**, avoiding bear traps and pitfalls along the way. The plan is a progression of stages or actions, and unsurprisingly is called the Seven Stage Sales Progression. It is the road map for highly successful selling. With a minimum of wastage and procrastination it puts the arrow dead centre of the sales bullseye.

Highly successful sales happen because the sales person makes the buying contact feel comfortable with saying 'Yes'. They build some early trust when they open the door (or pick up the phone) in the critical Initial Approach phase. They don't hurry or pressurize. They conduct specific preparation prior to engaging the buying contact and refine their approach so that when they initiate it, it wins credibility, attention and interest. They don't Feature Dump products and services. They ask a series of highly polished questions over time (short or long period) designed to engage the buying contact and go beyond dictated wants to specific needs. They uncover issues and 'problems' and the physical impact of them; normally (but not exclusively) a cost or costs.

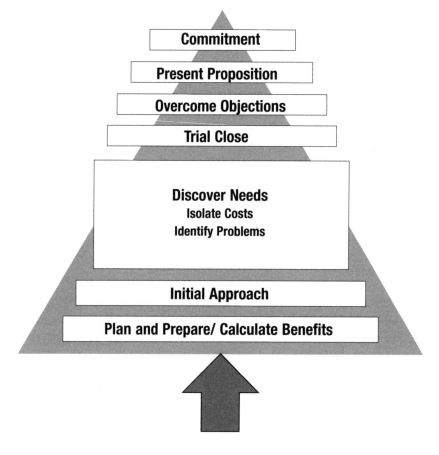

And then they uncover others. On completion of the information-gathering phase they conversationally Trial Close to validate interest and draw out objections. Then they handle the objections in a non-confrontational and skilful manner. Then (unlike other less successful sales persons) they present their proposition based on established and agreed **needs**. And then they conversationally seek to move the sale onto the next stage of the process: perhaps a demo, or benchmarking, or indeed the negotiation – they close for a meaningful commitment.

THE SALES PROGRESSION

Some sales people that I've met say that selling is a personal business, where sales people find a style and skills that suit them. While this is true in some limited respects, it is fraught with dangers – many of which will be explored in this book. My experience says that the closer you stay to this progression the faster and more predictably the sale happens. Let's look at each stage first and then we'll look at why.

GET IN SHAPE

The Progression is based on a triangle – the classic shape in selling. We always begin at the bottom with a broad base of question asking and information gathering. This develops over time with the questions narrowing until we ask the ultimate one: 'Will you?'

PLAN AND PREPARE/CALCULATE BENEFITS

Picking up a telephone or knocking on a door **blind** can be a recipe for disaster. There are many sales people who make plenty of calls in a day without really knowing what they are going to say much beyond introducing themselves and *maybe* asking a leading question.

And then again, I know plenty of sales people who will not initiate an approach to a prospect without first having visited their website and done some 'Research'. Of course, there is a downside to placing too much stock on website information: often, websites portray what the company wants you to think, which might not necessarily be 100 per cent accurate... Also, all of this surfing burns valuable selling time, and sometimes it can be used as an excuse: *If I research for long enough it'll be time to go home!* I agree it's good to be prepared, but in the right way. (We focus on preparing in the right way by working out how you are going to get the door open in Chapter 4.)

However, to *begin* the preparation process we can ask ourselves questions like: what kind of problems have we found in this sort of operation in the past? How have we provided a solution to those problems? What benefits have we provided? What value did they represent to the customer? Based on past experience, what is the sales potential of this prospect likely to be? How will we get the door open? What's going to get them interested?

THE INITIAL APPROACH

How we initiate the approach is one of the two biggest causes of failed sales. It all lives and dies right here: in order to carry the sale forward past the initial 'I don't want to be cold called' objection, we have to grab **handfuls** of **attention** and **interest**. Without it the approach will die!

Many sales people notoriously use closing at this stage; closing in the opening moments of the call! 'Hi, I'd like to come and talk to you about our fabulous money-saving products – when is good for you?' This automatically creates rejection as the sales person is trying to pressure the prospect into a commitment that came at them like a linebacker from the Washington Redskins! Others start talking about products and services: 'I'm just ringing to talk to you about our new Premium Service.' This triggers the shut-up-so-I-can-hang-up reaction! Others claim to be 'just updating the database'. This triggers the database-fantasy reaction where the prospect visualizes beating the sales person to death with it! If you are using these approaches, like John you will be making more calls than a double-glazing sales person on go-go juice without a 'stop' button.

This stage is **critical** to our success. If we don't carefully construct the right approach we will end up spending huge amounts on phone bills or shoe leather, only to see a desperately poor return on our time investment.

Chapter 4 is also dedicated to the Initial Approach.

DISCOVER NEEDS

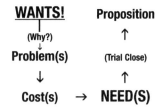

This is typically the stage where sales people ask a range of questions to identify product and service fit. As soon as they find one (or *perhaps* more) opportunity they begin the selling presentation. Frequently sales people focus on the wants of the buying contact: 'We want four Model 4000 Vortex Suction Machines delivered within six weeks at a price of no more than £30k per unit.' Cascade Sales people are not interested in the want. They are interested in the 'Why?'

Our job is to go beyond the wants and find out what is driving or causing them. Only through doing this can we start to uncover the problems that our proposition may be able to solve. But don't stop there. Many sales people will want to start presenting a proposition at this point but it is much too soon. A sales person may see a problem but a buying contact may not, or if they do they will not see it on the same scale. Before we start selling anything we have to help the buying contact to see the cost or costs. The bigger the better! Only when they have seen the significant cost of a problem will they potentially see the need. So, to positively begin the sales process: to get a prospect to consider talking to us or meeting with us or buying from us, we have to go beyond wants and start uncovering problems. Is this easy? It's probably one of the most difficult parts of the Progression for many sales people. Chapter 5 will provide us with technique to unearth genuine problems.

TRIAL CLOSE

I have spent literally hundreds of hours sitting in on both telephone sales calls and face-to-face sales visits to assess the process and skills being employed by sales people, and it's always fascinating to see what they have in common. Everybody knows the Trial Close because it is in everyone's speech pattern, but many sales people fatally do not use it at this point in the Progression. Answer me this: what normally happens when a sales person has done their digging and identified a range of opportunities to sell their products or services? They start presenting them, right? 'I've found out all the areas where our product is a good fit; now all I've got to do is demonstrate the relevant features and benefits, and it's a sure thing!' There is only one thing worse than this: 'I've found **one** area where our product is a good fit.'

Welcome to Cause-of-Failed-Sales Number Two. The cause is the failure to Trial Close before presenting the proposition. The sales person finds out what the prospect wants and then they show them that they can have it. All they forget to do is find out if they are genuinely interested.

Ever had a sale that started out hot, straight and true? Everything was looking good until you presented the product and started closing for commitment? Then the prospect started saying things like 'I need to think about it' or 'Why don't you put something in writing to us?' You walked away bemusedly scratching your head trying to figure out what the hell went wrong. Ever been there? Before you start presenting and closing, the Trial Close is designed to draw out the 'No'. Now I know that you might be reading this with incredulity: 'What is this Anyon guy – *crazy?* Why the hell would I want to hear "No"? I hear that often enough as it is!' And I understand. Let's face it – all you really want to hear is 'Yes', mainly because 'No' is the ultimate rejection and who needs that, right? Also, some of the best things that have happened to you in your life have happened right after someone else has said 'Yes'. However, the Trial Close is used here as the qualification close: it is designed to qualify, **validate** or check their interest, prior to proposition and closing. This is done specifically to bring out the hidden objections that you haven't uncovered yet.

If you do not uncover those potential objections now, when you reach the other end of the sale, make the huge presentation and are in the end-zone closing like your life depended on it, it will all unravel and you'll never know why it went wrong.

The Trial Close begins with 'If' or 'So if' and is (not surprisingly) also known as the So If Close. Additionally it is called the Half Nelson as, like the wrestling hold of the same name, it is very difficult to escape from. Also it is called the Summary Trial Close, used to summarize a range of points before closing on them. Here are some examples:

- So if we could help you reduce operational downtime, would you be interested?
- If we could help you increase production efficiency, would you want to talk about it?
- If I bought the lunch would you be able to spend thirty minutes with me?
- Roger: if we could help you make some of these operational issues go

away, would you be interested in seeing how?

– Roger: if we could help you improve productivity, reduce distribution downtime and improve production flow, would you be interested?

– If I said you had a beautiful body, would you hold it against me? (This last example is included to warn against the use of very well-known and overused Trial Closing).

The rule with this (and every other question that we ask in selling) is then to use the Pregnant Pause: **shut up** and let them answer. Give them some thinking time and some breathing space. Sales people are often uncomfortable with silence and so jump into the gap and volunteer answers that might not have been on the prospect's wish-list, but are now! If I had a euro for every time I have heard a sales person **not** shut up after a question or Trial Close, I would be the owner of a small but perfectly formed bank in sunny Switzerland. The Trial Close is used specifically to unearth objections at this point in the Progression, because if you don't they will remain hidden and unanswered until the end of the sale at which time they will sink the Good Ship Sell-a-Lot.

We discuss Trial Closing in more detail in Chapter 5.

OVERCOME OBJECTIONS

The mandate in Cascade Selling is that you have to draw out and overcome as many objections as possible (all of them would be nice) **before** you present your proposition. This is an essential skill and needs to be executed with talent and care, so I'm always a little surprised when I find sales people meeting objections head on in a manner guaranteed to promote conflict! An unbelievably common example of this is:

Buying contact: 'We don't need any of your products thank you.'
Sales person: 'Are you sure?'

Or:

Buying contact: 'We don't need any of your products thank you.'
Sales person: 'Why not?'

There are problems with some of the traditional methods of *overcoming* objections. We discuss some useful and practical skills in Chapter 6.

PRESENT PROPOSITION

When you have reached the point where you have asked through Trial Closing: 'Look Roger; if we could help you significantly reduce the amount that you spend on pre-production prototypes and can help you get your product to market in a lot less time, would you be interested?' and Roger says: 'Absolutely!' then it's time to show him how you would achieve these benefits by presenting the proposition.

In Cascade Selling there are broadly speaking two different things that we sell. First, there is the normal product and service proposition where we match specific product and service benefits to established and agreed needs. We prove each benefit with the relevant product feature: 'The way in which we remove the system-crash issue is by ensuring that there is always a 20 per cent memory buffer thus giving the platform the necessary room to function effectively.' And second, there is what *really* makes the sale happen which we cover in Chapter 7.

COMMITMENT

Once we have demonstrated the proposition we then move the sale forwards and gain commitment by closing. Closing should not be a nail-bitingly manipulative coercion on our part. It should merely be a natural and conversational extension of the sale. It might be to gain a commitment to an order, but equally it could be to move forward to benchmarking, a demonstration or perhaps to the financial negotiation. There are practical examples of closing in the latter stages of the book.

THE POWER BEHIND THE THRONE

Why do some sales fail? Why do some sales people have to make ten presentations to get one order? In many cases it's not that they don't have structure in what they do; it's more the case that they don't have a carefully refined one designed to get the best results.

The Seven Stage Sales Progression has been designed specifically for Cascade Selling, and we have only just scratched the surface in bringing it to life. There are a number of key reasons why it is so powerful and effective:

– It goes against a high percentage of common sales practice. Many sales pitches begin with **the kiss of death to selling**. They begin with a **Feature Dump** presentation to tell the prospect all about us and our products. This **fatal approach** causes a number of things:
  • General presentations or pitches are B-O-R-I-N-G!
  • With so many different people in the room, how will you present something substantial and interesting for everyone?
  • How will you know who is actually decision-relevant?
  • Once you have shown a buying contact what you've got, they will think

that they are in possession of enough information with which to decide on whether or not they want it. Often they don't.

• How many specific needs can you discover when you're making a **Feature Dump** presentation? Trick question: the answer is **none**.

– Presenting the proposition is delayed until we have uncovered their needs and can provide a **qualified** proposition to them.

– The Sales Progression minimizes resistance and objections from a buying contact by delaying the initial close until their wants, needs, concerns and problems have been established. It creates a climate in which they feel less threatened and more comfortable with saying 'Yes'.

– This model is elastic. In real terms the first two stages can take moments and 'Needs Discovery' can take minutes, hours, weeks, months, or in some cases even years! It will expand and contract depending upon the needs of the sales user and the complexity of the sale.

– Sales people will be involved with as many Progressions as there are buying contacts, and will be at different levels at different times. Movement up **and** down a Progression is also common; for example, if Trial Closing is not productive it is a good idea to return to Discover Needs.

– Buying contacts don't like surprises and they are suspicious of sales people; there is always the fear of manipulation to contend with here. The Progression walks them through a step-by-step process that is transparent at all times. It doesn't try force feeding them with product-based mush. It gives them the opportunity to take a leading role in a logical series of stages that conclude in a positive but non-pressurized commitment. *Analytical* buying contacts love this logical process.

<u>A</u>TTENTION

<u>I</u>NTEREST

<u>D</u>ESIRE

<u>A</u>CTION

– It fulfils probably the oldest acronym in selling: AIDA. In our technologically dominated world anything old is deemed to be obsolete but this **old is gold**. AIDA defines the four stages of the sales process. You can pronounce it like a 1940s lady's name or like Giuseppe Verdi's Italian opera. What it says is that when initiating a cold approach at whatever level of decision-relevant authority, the first thing that you have got to do is to positively get the attention of the person to whom you are selling. Next you have to very quickly turn that attention into interest. Once you've got them interested you have to make them want whatever it is they think you have to offer, and then you've got to get them to do something about it: cause them to act in your favour!

'OF ALL THE GIN JOINTS IN ALL THE TOWNS IN ALL THE WORLD…'

You know what it's like. It's the end of a long hard day and you manage to sneak away from the office a little earlier than the ridiculous time at which you normally leave. As you leave the building your head turns involuntarily to Rick's Café Américain just down the street and you decide to treat yourself! As you approach it you can see that the bar is open but it's still early; most of the chairs are on the tables. You walk into the cool dimly lit interior and throw your case and jacket onto the bar. This is no ordinary bar. Of all the bars in all the world that you have stood at, this is the longest, most beautifully carved piece of highly polished mahogany. As you look into the devoid-of-customers gloom the mahogany just seems to go on for ever. From the darkness Raoul appears like an apparition, recognizes you and says: 'The usual?' With a nod of your head you confirm and within moments the first drink of the (early) evening arrives. For many, but particularly for sales people, this is a special moment. It doesn't matter what your poison is – it's just the way that it hits the spot. Back in the days of cowboys and such they would say that a beer would cut the dust from your throat. In the days of the 21st century Business Western (still a few cowboys around but less dust) the first drink of the evening either cuts away the B.S. or de-stresses the user like a coiled spring on muscle relaxant.

The glass that contains your Martini is chilled to the point that the freezing dew on the outside of it is sliding off with all the haste of molasses in wintertime. As you take the first sip, trying desperately not to conduct nasal brain-removal-surgery with the skewered olive, it's like someone pushed the degauss button on your brain and everything's going to be alright. Tomorrow *will* be another day!

As you wrap yourself in the Joy of Cocktails you notice that you were wrong. Down at the end of the bar you spy a shape in the darkness, which must be another customer enjoying their drink. You don't give it another thought and return to your liquid fun but, as is the way with these things, in time you look back. Half-a-dozen more glances and as your eyes become accustomed to the light you realize that this is probably the most attractive person that you have ever seen.

Now imagine that you're single. The little worm inside your brain (Martini not Tequila) tells you that the person in front of you is the man or woman of your dreams. You **know** that if you don't go over and say *something* you will probably never see this person again and will doubtless regret it for the rest of your natural life. Five minutes later and with another glass of liquid fortification provided by Raoul down the hatch, you tentatively and a little nervously approach the person in the shadows. Yes, wait for it: this story does have a point.

Now you **know** that on approaching the prospect your enemy is rejection. That's where the nerves come from. You are going to have to say or do something to positively get their **attention,** and if it isn't good they will **blow you out!** Men are **really talented** here – they use such classic and highly persuasive one-liners as 'If I said you had a beautiful body would you hold it against me?' They also believe that putting their trousers on their head is in some way helpful here. No really – I've no idea why!

Then you are very quickly going to have to turn that attention into interest. Laughter works well here, but not **at** you; **with** you would be nice. After that at some point you are going to need to get the other person to want (**desire**) whatever it is that they think you have to offer (whatever that is). And then you're going to need to get them to say 'Yes' to something (**action**)... **Obviously** this will be to joining you for a drink, getting their phone number or perhaps agreeing to a date of some kind.

So AIDA is not just a description of the sales process – it also describes (in reasonable detail) the human courtship ritual. But both are based on the same thing: the desire to sell something to someone else.

In a commercial context we get the attention of the buying contact when we initiate the approach. Their interest is gained during Needs Discovery. We ask skilful questions, and in answering they hear the thing they love the sound of the most: their own voice. Desire is produced using the Trial Close: 'If we could make this problem go away, would you be interested?' And action is catalysed through closing for a commitment.

Now that the Progression has provided us with purpose and structure we are in a position to populate it with all of the critical detail, function and skills that comprise Cascade Selling. But before we do anything else we need to focus on the toughest nut to crack, the biggest challenge that we face in selling, **the** most important thing in sales.

You'll need to turn the page!

CHAPTER 2

STEP 2
AND THE MOST IMPORTANT THING IN SELLING IS?

We could play a guessing game on this one for hours, couldn't we? What is the most important thing in selling? There are hundreds of possible answers, all of which would have some merit because selling isn't exactly a pushover occupation: everything from gaining attention and interest to handling tough objections is difficult. But from my perspective the toughest nut to crack, the frequently unfathomable puzzle is… the people. The people to whom we sell can be by far the biggest challenge. Get the interaction right and you earn the right to have a sales conversation. Build a little trust and they might just start buying into what you're saying. Get the relationship thing right and you stand a much stronger chance of keeping them as a customer. The way in which we interface with the people to whom we sell is critical to our success.

There are several models in existence that give us a psychological basis for successful interaction with others. Over the years I have percolated the models, the research and the studies utilizing the best ideas from each, and taken shortcuts where necessary, purely for ease of use. I have tried to avoid the highly involved or complex versions because in Cascade Selling, if our *human interface skills* are critical to the outcome, then we need ones that are easy to learn, develop, remember **and** apply.

Interface Skills is without question one of the most powerful business tools you will ever meet! In a practical way it focuses on unlocking the mysteries of human relationships. In 21st century sales this means the relationships that we strive to develop with prospects and customers to win brand new business in economical timescales, and then lock the business in over the long term.

THE INTERFACE SKILLS

Look in the mirror. Do you have tight and productive working relationships with all of your customers? On approaching prospects do you **automatically find their wavelength?** Or are there contacts that you just can't work out? You never quite seem to crack the compatibility thing. On the other hand are there contacts that frustrate, bore or intimidate you? If any of these is the case, let's take a look at the reasons why. We are going to peel an onion layer by layer to the heart of the matter to comprehend the human condition; to understand what makes people tick in a sales environment.

THE INTERFACE SKILLS MATRIX

The Interface Skills are based on a simple human truth. Do you agree with the following statements?

People buy from people. I'm not interested in the internet here. Do you agree that people buy from people? Your answer *should* be 'Yes'.

What about: people buy from people whom they either like or trust. Do you agree with this statement? If you're in sales your answer once again *should* be 'Yes'.

Try this: people buy from people whom they either like or trust because they perceive them to be like them. Do you believe that people buy from others who are like them? Perhaps because they have the same shared experience, the same values or indeed the same specialist or social language? Do you agree with that? Once again your answer *should* be 'Yes'.

Put all of that another way. How about: birds of a feather flock together? What do you think of that? Well, let's take a look.

THE INTERFACE SKILLS MATRIX

From this point forwards please do not assume that you understand the meaning of any of the words that you will see in the pictures until I have defined them for you. For example, Driver has nothing whatsoever to do with automotive vehicles!

This section is the psychobabble bit but don't worry – it becomes very practical very quickly. Take a look at the matrix. Out there in the world: Europe, Scandinavia, North and South America, Australia and New Zealand, but not in the Middle and Far East (because of the extremes of cultural diversity), there are four styles of people. They are called: the Driver, the Analytical, the Amiable and the Expressive. Each of these people is governed by three axes:

The horizontal axis says 'Assertiveness'. Assertiveness is the degree to which they are demanding of other people: low and high.

The vertical axis says 'Responsiveness'. Responsiveness is the degree to which they are giving of themselves to other people: low and high.

The third axis is the horizontal dividing line; above the line these types are logical: thinkers. Below the line they are emotional: feelers.

Out there in the world there are four types of people. Each of them is colour-coded.

DEFINING THE TYPES

Defining the Driver

Their colour code is red. What does red represent in our society? Stop! Danger! Warning! Drivers are highly demanding of other people and not very giving of themselves in return. Above the line they are logical; they are not interested in emotion. They deal in fact, they deal in proof – they want results. Drivers are in control. They are time and attention poor. They **don't** suffer fools gladly. The cardinal sin that you don't commit with a Driver is to **waste their time.**

Real world: think about all of the businesses out there. In a normal or typical company structure, perhaps like yours, what job title do Drivers gravitate to? You can find them in lots of areas but in the one where you get a massively high percentage of Drivers the norm is chief executive officer (CEO), managing director (MD) or director.

✓CEO
✓MD
✓Director

Defining the Analytical

Their colour code is blue. A pale blue: cool or ice blue. Many people see the Analytical as quite emotionless or very much a cold fish; cold-blooded, no passion: the clinician. Analyticals are not demanding of other people and not giving of themselves either. Above the line, they are logical. Analyticals are all about thinking, understanding, gathering facts, fine details, numbers and data. They love empirical evidence. When you talk to an Analytical they will say 'Why?', 'How does it work?', 'Has it been trialled?', 'How long has it been trialled for?', 'How many users has it had?', 'Where are the feedback reports?'…

When an Analytical buys a car they don't go to a showroom – they are not interested in meeting an 'enthusiastic' sales person and being given a glossy brochure. An Analytical sends off to Volvo for the workshop manual or for the production manual. They want to know data like the variance in the tolerance of paint thickness, measured in microns, across the fuel filler cap compared to, say, the roof.

They want chapter and verse; they want detail. An Analytical doesn't make snap judgements or decisions. You can't *persuade* them or sell to them because they will see right through your argument. They gather all the information, they process it mentally and in their own time they form a judgement.

Real world: to what job title in a company might you expect an Analytical to gravitate? Finance, IT and engineering are quite normal for Analyticals.

✓Finance	✓CEO
✓IT	✓MD
✓Engineering	✓Director

Defining the Amiable

Their colour code is grey. What does grey mean in our society? One person thinks that grey is dull or boring, but it is actually the neutral colour, neither black nor white.

Be careful. Amiable does not mean what it means in common English usage. It does not mean having a pleasant disposition, friendly and good-natured. The best definition that I have heard to describe the Amiable was from a Swedish delegate, who said that it means 'unsure'. Amiables are not very demanding of other people, but hugely giving of themselves. Below the line, they are highly emotional. They genuinely care about you, your life and how you feel. Amiables really care about the people around them. For them the job is unimportant, it's all about the personal relationships.

Amiables, however, are very rarely found in sales – why? Because they can't stand under the spotlight: they fear and avoid conflict and the pressure that causes it. If you put an Amiable face-to-face with an angry customer the Amiable will withdraw feeling threatened and intimidated. If you put an Amiable on the other side of the desk from a sales person who is trying to convince them of something, they will wriggle and squirm to try to get out from under the pressure. You might even force them to say 'Yes', but they will change their mind later. Amiables are probably the most reliable people in a business but you don't find them in the front line.

Real world: what job title will you find them in? Often you find them in the support functions or back office. They can also be found in HR – but not management; they stay in the background avoiding interaction with people who will create challenge and conflict.

✓Finance	✓CEO
✓IT	✓MD
✓Engineering	✓Director
✓Support	
✓Back Office	
✓HR	

Defining the Expressive

Their colour code is green but not just any old boring green; it's bright green – '**go**' green. Expressive does what it says on the tin. Expressive means expressive. Expressives are hugely demanding of other people and hugely giving of themselves – all at the same time. Expressives are below the line and are highly emotional. They aren't interested in the fine detail like the Analytical; what they are interested in is having fun. They don't care about the numbers, the facts and the details; B-O-R-I-N-G! These people are the life and soul of the party. Expressives get bored easily. When they get bored they will decide to do something rash and spontaneous like buy a car. What kind of car? Well a sports car, of course! And the colour? Red, of course, because it's expressive! Don't bore me with administration; give me something exciting to do.

Real world: what job do you think Expressives congregate to? The absolute classic is sales, and the creative functions like PR and advertising.

✓Finance	✓CEO
✓IT	✓MD
✓Engineering	✓Director
✓Support	✓Sales
✓Back Office	✓PR
✓HR	✓Advertising

MULTIPLE STYLES

The interesting thing here is that there are four types, but very few people are just one type. Some people are one type, some are a combination of two, some of three, but there is no such thing as a person with a combination of all four styles. Why? Because of the conflicts that exist between them.

CONFLICTS EXPERIMENT – TRY THIS!

Get a scrap of paper and a pen. Write four words in a column on the left side: 'Me', 'Boss', 'Best' and 'Worst'.

Me	▷ Expressive
Boss	▷ Driver
Best	▷ Expressive
Worst	▷ Analytical

Next to the word 'Me' write the style that you think you are most like in the workplace. This might be in the office or perhaps in front of customers. Or put it another way: write down what you think your **Dominant Style** is at work.

Next, write the style that you think your boss is most like at work: his or her Dominant Style.

Then, think about the best relationship that you ever had at work. This can be in the past or present. It could be with a colleague or a customer. Write the Dominant Style of that person down next to 'Best'.

Finally, think about the worst relationship that you've ever had at work. You know the one. You two have just never seen eye to eye, always had daggers drawn. Once again it could be a colleague or a customer, or perhaps even a supplier! Write the Dominant Style of the worst relationship that you've ever had at work next to 'Worst'.

Now, do you remember that I said there is no such thing as one person with all four styles in them? The reason for this is because of the conflicts. As we go through them, think about the comparison that you have just created.

THE CONFLICTS

The Driver and the Analytical

These two get on quite well and this is no surprise as most CEOs come from a financial background and so they typically have a strong analytical side. Drivers tend to see Analyticals as an aid, workhorse, asset or resource.

Analyticals recognize that they have this in common and also acknowledge the status of the Driver. The Driver after all is in charge. However, Analyticals will not allow themselves to be pressured, intimidated or coerced **even** by a CEO Driver.

The Analytical and the Amiable

The Analytical thinks the Amiable is okay but so needlessly emotional.

The Amiable thinks the Analytical is all right, but they just don't seem to care about people.

The Amiable and the Expressive

The Amiable and the Expressive is an interesting one. The Amiable either finds the Expressive very scary because of the pressure that they put them under in a selling environment or as co-workers the Amiable can find the Expressive a bit wacky and quite entertaining.

The Expressive finds the Amiable as frustrating as hell. Whenever they try to close them into a commitment they avoid it at all costs. No matter how much pressure the Expressive puts the Amiable under, the Amiable will always wriggle and squirm and avoid it.

The Expressive and the Driver

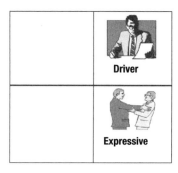

The Expressive can find the Driver quite overpowering and, at times, quite intimidating. The Driver is the CEO who is always banging on the desk and saying to the sales person: 'Get to the point and stop wasting my time!' No matter how much charm the Expressive applies, it never seems to work on the Driver.

Drivers hate Expressives – CEOs hate sales people. The Driver is interested in facts, proof and results but the Expressive never provides these things. All the Expressive tries to do is paint the Driver a picture in technicolour, get them excited about the idea, and then let's go get a beer.

The Analytical and the Expressive

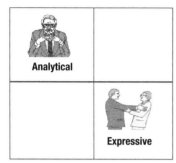

The Analytical can't stand the Expressive. All the Analytical wants is facts, the data and all the Expressive is interested in, as with the Driver, is to paint a picture in technicolour, get them excited about the idea, and then let's go get a beer. The Expressive finds the Analytical B-O-R-I-N-G! How many more numbers do you **need?** How dull is **that?**

The Amiable and the Driver

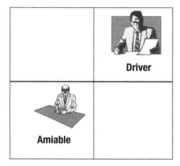

The Amiable is intimidated in the extreme by the Driver because he is always putting them under pressure for results.

The Driver thinks: 'Why do we employ this person? What positive impact do they have on our results? How do they contribute to the financial performance of the business?'

EXERCISE: FAST ANALYSIS – IDENTIFY WHICH STYLES ARE PRESENT

The next thing we are going to do is learn to identify the different styles in a person. **For this we need a victim, someone you know very well or perhaps even you.** The first thing you are going to decide is which styles are present in your choice of subject and then we're going to see which style is the Dominant. Remember, your subject will have at least one style visible, and a maximum of three.

For the sake of this exercise let's call the subject Sam (male or female). Think about Sam in the workplace. It doesn't matter how large or small the amount, but:

Is there any evidence of Driver in Sam? Yes or no?
Is there any evidence of Analytical in Sam? Yes or no?
Is there any evidence of Amiable in Sam? Yes or no?
Is there any evidence of Expressive in Sam? Yes or no?

Now take each of the (three maximum) styles that you have identified and decide on a percentage for each. Remember that the total will need to add up to 100 per cent. If you think you have someone with all four styles, either you have made a mistake in which case you'll need to go back and do the analysis again, or you have selected a **Derf.**

FRED, FERD OR DERF

A couple of years ago I delivered a Key Account Management training course for a company in the UK selling medical equipment to the National Health Service.

It was wintertime and I arrived at the hotel venue long after dark. I had driven there in icy and treacherous road conditions, having nearly been run off the road several times by other motorists. By the time I arrived at about 9.00 p.m. I was frazzled.

I checked in and then went into the bar on the way to my room. I walked straight into a group of a dozen people who, it transpired, were my delegates for the next few days. The client greeted me and introduced me to the sales team. It was like standing in a wedding line being introduced to them one at a time. The only difference was that I was still holding my luggage and there wasn't a bride in sight.

The last sales person in the line walked up to me and, shaking my hand, said enthusiastically: 'Hi! My name is Fred, Ferd and Derf!'

I was in no mood for jokes! I had just driven the dangerous 200 miles or whatever it was to get here and now I had to deal with this joker? I wondered what the hell was going on. But, of course, I just shook him by the hand. I went and dumped my bags in my room and we all got together for dinner and a few drinks.

During the course of the evening I asked a few of Fred's colleagues: 'What is the Fred, Ferd and Derf thing all about? What is it: some kind of joke?'

'Gosh no,' they told me with concern. 'No, he genuinely believes that he is three different people and slips from one personality to the next without knowing he's doing it!'

Later in the evening I sat down with Fred and, just as they had said he would, he slipped from the Fred personality to the Ferd and then finally the Derf and then back again without apparently knowing he was doing it. And in those three personas I saw a mixture of all four Interface Styles.

Of course, he was a nightmare to train as I had to rephrase everything four times. So, here's the exception to the rule: there is no such thing as someone who has all four styles in them, unless, of course, that person is a bit behaviourally confused. And then I guess anything could happen in the next half hour!

ISOLATING THE DOMINANT STYLE

What you should have now is one style that is the largest percentage. This is called the Dominant. So, once we have identified what we think the Dominant is, this is the style upon which we focus. Be advised that the Dominant Style can and will change depending on circumstances and stimuli. For example, a Driver might become Analytical if you give them something interesting to think about or an Expressive might become a Driver if you present them with too much detail, or stop them from having fun. Another point to consider is that people often have a different style at home or socially, compared to their Dominant in the workplace. This style is known as the **Natural Style** and is the one to which they default in the absence of workplace pressures.

Next: let's say you have a Driver prospect. If you are going to pitch to them on a cold call by telephone, what do you think is the most effective style in which to sell to them?

At the beginning of this chapter I asked you if you believe the following: people buy from people whom they either like or trust because they perceive them to be like them. Put another way, birds of a feather flock together.

THRASHING ABOUT IN THE POOL, DRUNK

When you go to a party 'Birds of a feather flock together' becomes really obvious: all of the CEOs head for the bar. They go straight past the Bacardi and the vodka in the speed rail, and root around at the back looking for the finest, the oldest and the most expensive cognac.

All of the financial people head for the kitchen. They find the jar of fresh coffee beans, tip them out onto the work surface and start *counting* them.

All of the marketing people strip the furniture out of the living room and take it up onto the flat roof where they build a whacky creation that's *in the sky, man.*

And the sales people abandon sense, sensibility, sobriety and their clothing and they all thrash about in the pool, drunk. Fabulous profession, sales!

In order to sell effectively to someone you have to sound like them. You have to act like them. You have to sell to them in the way that they want to be sold to!

So what am I going to suggest that you do here? Am I going to suggest that you change your personality to suit the people to whom you are selling? Be careful – you can't change your personality. Not without **months** of intensive electroshock treatment. And at the end of that you might just have lost interest in selling. What you can do however is *modify your behaviour*. There should be no great difficulty here. Sales people are supposed to be chameleons – changing their skin colour (behaviour) to suit their environment. Matching their Interface Style to that of the person to whom they are selling.

WHAT'S IMPORTANT TO THE STYLES

So far then we have established that if you are going to pitch to a Driver prospect, say, on a cold call by telephone, the most effective style in which to sell to them is their own. Before we physically define the most effective selling behaviour for each style it's important to know what they need to get from the interaction; how we need to make them feel.

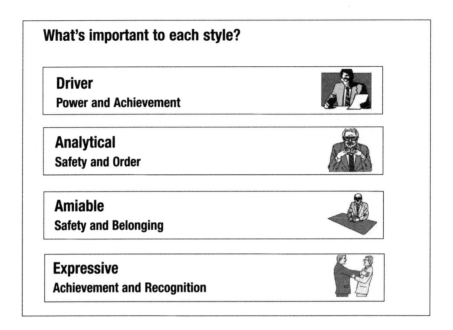

What's important to each style?

Driver
Power and Achievement

Analytical
Safety and Order

Amiable
Safety and Belonging

Expressive
Achievement and Recognition

Drivers want power. Status and achievement are important to them. When selling to a Driver a sales person has to make them feel powerful and make them feel that they are getting something of real value from the interaction.

Analyticals don't like risks. For them it's about safety: safety from wrong or bad decisions. And it's about order: they love being taken through a Cascade Sales Progression by a structured sales person because they can see exactly where they are going.

Amiables care. It's about emotional safety and belonging in a relationship that they care about, in this case with the sales person.

Expressives want achievement and to be recognized for it. You have to make them feel good.

HOW TO SELL TO THE STYLES

How do we deal with these styles productively and proactively in a sales environment, and skilfully enough to bring about the things that are important to them? For this we refer to the study of Non-Verbal Communication or Body Language. What is the rule in body language? In order to breed mutuality in a relationship there are noteworthy occasions when you should mirror the body language of the other person. This means copying their body position and movements but not identically and in a subtle way. We also need to emulate their vocal pattern and tone – to sound like them.

With Interface Skills we mirror the Interface Style, the key behaviours of the other person:

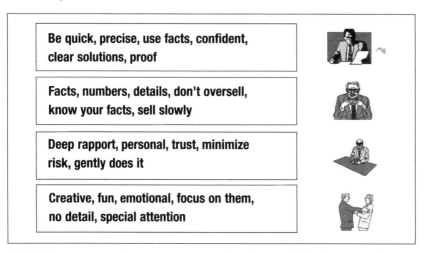

Be quick, precise, use facts, confident, clear solutions, proof

Facts, numbers, details, don't oversell, know your facts, sell slowly

Deep rapport, personal, trust, minimize risk, gently does it

Creative, fun, emotional, focus on them, no detail, special attention

With Drivers: get to the point! Be precise: hit them with the facts. You have to **be** confident. You have to **sound** confident. Match their verbal pattern – if they are using a dominating tone then you should use one that's similar. Present clear arguments and solutions and back them up with proof.

With Analyticals: you can't sell to an Analytical. You have to feed them with the facts, numbers and detail. They govern the pace. Know your facts and convince them slowly.

With Amiables: it's all about building deep rapport and friendship. Selling has to wait. With these people you wear kid gloves and treat them very carefully. You have to be prepared to share relationships and family – yours and theirs.

With Expressives: they are creative. They want the interaction to be emotional and fun. Give them lots of special attention; forget the details. Paint them a picture in technicolour. Get them excited about the idea! They love meeting in out-of-the-office places (bar, beach, park or a museum) and the whole corporate entertainment thing.

SHOW ME THE MONEY

Let's look at an actual example of the Interface Skills in action. The style that many sales people find difficult to emulate is that of a Driver. Part of the reason for this is the perceived difference in status. The CEO sees an irritating and subservient sales person and the sales person sees a dominating tyrant with God-like status. Hardly a recipe for harmony or productivity, is it?

Some time ago I attended an initial appointment (IA) with a prospect based in Cambridge (UK). The meeting was with the **Scandanavian CEO**. From our previous telephone conversation, I had already identified that he was an absolutely *classic* Driver: 'Get to the point, don't waste my time, show me the money.' I had uncovered two potential service sales opportunities so I took a colleague with me who specialized in one of the services.

It took my colleague an hour to get to our meeting point. It then took us four hours to travel cross-country by car to the prospect's premises, which was a barn conversion in a village just outside Cambridge. We arrived in reception 15 minutes before the appointed meeting time of 11.30 a.m. The prospect kept us waiting in reception for 45 minutes. Eventually he breezed out of his office and, without saying a word of greeting, crooked a finger at us in a 'Follow me' gesture and walked out of the building. We followed. He carried on walking. It was a lovely summer's day and he was obviously enjoying the sun. He walked across the car park, up a lane and into the entrance to a field, stopping at a five-bar gate, whereupon he began stroking the head of a horse that had approached. Eventually we caught up with him.

He said, in a firm and unwavering voice: 'My schedule has changed. You've got five minutes.'

This was a little surprising. On the telephone we had agreed a one-hour timeframe for the meeting. Also, we appeared to have dispensed with the social pleasantries like 'Hello. Good morning. Nice to meet you' and all of that apparent waste of words. Additionally, without any time spent in the meeting we had already committed to a total of 18 hours of collective travelling time.

I have met sales people who start frothing at the mouth if they are kept waiting in Reception by a buying contact. It offends their more delicate sensibilities; it is an affront to their dignity! I have worked with others who would be totally bemused by the long walk of silence to the field. Some would find the snorting nag a little off-putting. I'm violently allergic to horses so others might find the running nose, swollen eyes and respiratory tract shut-down a bit of a distraction. The time pressure is too much for some sales people to bear as well. They immediately and automatically Feature Dump their products and services: 'Well this is the range of products that we do and these are our services and we were hoping to talk to you about how they might fit into your business…'

Driver gets bored, meeting ends in three minutes not five and you are never granted an audience again. Whilst it is true that sometimes you do only have five minutes, every sales person has heard those words and in some cases has still been in conversation an hour later. Feature Dumping is not an option, in **any** sale – so there is only one other thing left to do. Better get the Driver's attention and interest. The only way that you are going to do that is by selling to them effectively based on their Interface Style.

I said, in a firm and unwavering fashion: 'That's good. Five minutes is all we need. If we were in a position to help you drive up the output from your sales team, would you be interested?'

'Yes,' he replied.

'And if we could also help you reduce your recruitment costs and timescales by a significant degree, would you be interested in that?' I continued.

'Yes,' he replied once more. The conversation continued beyond the allotted five minutes.

THE INTERFACE SKILLS IN SIMPLE TERMS

If you are interested in highly successful selling it is critical that you are able to deal with buying contacts on their own level. Classically, many sales people are unsuccessful dealing with CEOs because they are so used to having their time wasted by unprepared sellers. **If you want to sell to a CEO you will have to learn to look, sound, think and act like them if you expect to get their attention and interest.** Forming a working understanding of the Interface Skills helps us achieve much closer relationships more quickly with our prospects and customers. With it we can breed greater mutuality.

In simple terms what it tells us is:

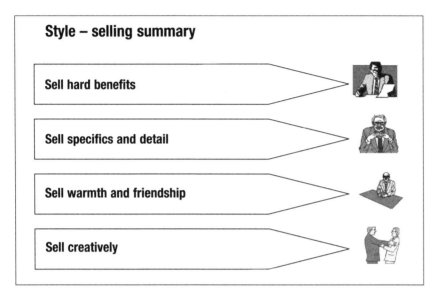

When dealing with **Drivers**, get to the point – hit them with the hard business benefit.

When dealing with **Analyticals**, make sure you present the detail.

When dealing with **Amiables**, make it personal: friendship first.

When dealing with **Expressives**, make it fun: relax and enjoy it.

INTERFACE STYLE QUICK RECOGNITION

In real life you don't really want to go through the long-winded process of writing down all of the styles and then allocating a percentage to identify the Dominant style of a prospect, right? I wouldn't either. How long do you think it takes to accurately identify the Interface Style of someone who you talk to for the very first time? Imagine that you cold call someone. They answer the telephone. From that moment how long does it take to accurately assess their Interface Style? I hear lots of answers to this question. They range from five to 120 seconds.

Finding out is a lot simpler than you'd think. Imagine that each of the four styles answers the telephone. Imagine what they would say and how they would say it:

The Driver: always abrupt, curt and to the point. Answers with their last name only: 'Anyon!'
The Analytical: in a very calm, controlled and emotionless voice: 'Hello. This is Greg Anyon speaking. How can I help you?'
The Expressive: loud, happy and smiling: 'Hi, this is Greg speaking. How can I help?'
The Amiable: warm and fluffy: 'Hello?'

In practical terms it only takes a few seconds to decide on the *Interface Style* with which we're dealing. It stands to reason then that if we are not dealing with a prospect or customer in their own style, getting their attention and interest is likely to be a bit challenging. Additionally, if we are planning an approach to a CEO prospect I think that it is safe enough to break Golden Sales Rule no. 749 about never assuming (because assumption is the mother of all screw-ups and it makes an ass of you and me), and assume that we are going to meet a Driver.

This being the case, whatever you say on an Initial Approach had better be delivered in the style of the person that you're approaching, right? Otherwise your call will be over quicker than an English summer.

CHAPTER 3

STEP 3
WHO ARE YOU GOING TO SELL TO?

The choice of who you are going to sell to is probably one of the single biggest influences on whether your high value sales approaches are successful or not. This choice also has a direct impact on the amount of time incurred in selling (the length of the sales cycle), and the quantity of resource that is either invested along the way, or burned. It will also dictate the amount of sales margin that you will be able to command from the end-zone negotiations. Additionally it can also be a dominant factor in how long you keep the customer for.

Not much riding on this one then!

ARE YOU SELLING TO MIDDLE MANAGEMENT?

Think about your existing customer relationships for a moment. How many of your buying relationships are with people at middle management level? When you target a prospect organization, how frequently do you approach someone in middle as opposed to senior management? Oh, I'm sure you've got senior management contacts but typically we tend to prospect and develop relationships below that level; often because senior people are difficult to gain access to and almost impossible to keep interested, right? And the larger the organization the worse it gets: have you ever tried getting hold of someone *really* big? What about Bill Clinton in the United States or the leader of the UK Conservative Party, David Cameron? Now while I don't know Bill Clinton I bet you I know someone who knows someone else that does (see Chapter 8). However, I know one of Mr Cameron's advisers. Does that help? It would if you were interested in selling to David Cameron and knew someone who knew me!

THE PATH OF LEAST SALES RESISTANCE

The classic sales method for approaching a prospect organization is often via the Path of Least Resistance. We sell, say, a complex technical product, so we initiate our approach with someone at middle level, who is likely to appreciate it or indeed recognize its benefits (we think): the technical manager perhaps or maybe the systems manager.

The minute we do this we voluntarily step into a cage and give someone else the keys. That person now has all the control and I guarantee that they will use it in their own service.

Sales people have found through history or experience that while the easiest point at which to penetrate a prospect organization in pursuit of the sale is at middle or lower level, what starts out as a potentially welcoming environment often ends up being the House of Pain. Let's weigh up the pros and cons:

The Pros
- These contacts rarely have personal assistants to screen them.
- They take some time to see us. It's worth going because what we have to say might be of some interest; we might trip over or create a sales opportunity.
- If they think your ideas are good ones, they might suggest them to someone more senior to sound out the likelihood of a purchase being authorized.
- And at least we have broken into the organization!

The Cons
- But they might not want to put you in touch with those more senior.
- If they do not have a formal purchase brief, they might be accused of wasting time and resource.
- They might feel that they will be passed over by the sales person, who naturally zeroes in on someone they believe to be more important.
- They know that the people senior to them do **not** respond well to having

sales people thrust upon them.

- If they don't introduce the sales person to people higher up the ladder, the sales person is stuck.
- And unless the middle- or lower-level person is very good at selling your products and services with the right benefits for those senior people, the sales person can spend months trying to progress the opportunity, to no avail.
- Basically, cover a pole in margarine and try climbing up it!

Frequently, the products and services that sales people provide are **ordered** or used by people at middle and junior levels of the organization but **financial sanction** is given by senior managers, especially for out-of-budget purchases.

Would it be fair to say then that being locked into middle management has disadvantages? Of course it does, especially in light of the other factor here:

THAT OLD FAVOURITE, THE DECISION-MAKING UNIT

Classically, in the happy land of selling the Decision-Making Unit (DMU) refers to all of the people involved in a buying organization who approve you as a supplier. This normally breaks down into loose subheadings of decision makers (directors, managers, etc.) and influencers (specifiers, supervisors, users, etc.). The DMU is often made up of more than one person in medium and large companies because so many departments and individuals are affected by a decision to purchase or change supplier. Sales people are frequently faced with selling to or dealing with one person, their entry-point contact – the tip of the DMU iceberg.

Having to deal with one member of the DMU, however, puts sales people at a huge disadvantage. Even if we are able to identify the things that are important to that individual, we are blind to the needs of the others. If we presented a proposition to one person when the very different needs of five have to be taken into account, then we just killed the sale! Along the way we also incurred a cost of sale that balloons based on an extended sales cycle, and then with no revenue at the end of it. How many of us as sales people have forecast the same business for six months, and then said it 'went away', when it might have been closed in one to two months? I'll put my hand up for that one if I'm dealing with one decision maker.

IDENTIFYING THE DMU SCALE

In gaining as comprehensive a picture as possible of the DMU there are a couple of critical questions that need answering.

When approaching a prospect organization, to whom should we sell to create the optimum conditions for a highly successful outcome? When seeking to protect our existing business from competitive threat, who should we sell to (or have strong working relationships with) to create the optimum conditions for a highly successful outcome?

The geometric shapes outlined below provide us with some graphically clear answers. They represent many of the most common compositions of the DMU, and in answering the questions above give us some useful indications for our Approach Strategy.

In the graphics, each of the dots represents a person. The number of people shown is purely illustrative. The lines represent the flow of communication or information:

Vertical Chains
In this classic hierarchy the CEO is normally at the top, followed down through layers of management to staff level.

Vertical Chains are very common and describe a situation where a decision has to be agreed by several levels of a hierarchy, each having input. In this kind of hierarchy the unpredictability of the chain is common as you can find Change Agents and Blockers scattered about all over the place.

Strategy: Who should we sell to? To get the maximum buy-in we need to approach as many members as possible.

Solo sales people penetrate the chain at middle management level, and struggle to fight their way to the top even if access has not been barred. Read on, however: there is a better way!

Team selling works well here: matching our CEO to theirs, our production director to theirs, like position to like position approaching as many different members as possible almost simultaneously.

Circles

A Circle describes a group of people (sometimes a committee) meeting to make or approve a decision. This may be a number of individuals of varying rank who come together on an equal footing to make a decision relevant to them all. Status is equal, and points of view are free-flowing.

These groups are often more creative, because the discussion process stimulates ideas. They tend to take more risks than an individual would, because the group gives its members a feeling of security. If it all goes wrong the group shares the blame.

Strategy: Who should we sell to? No single individual appears more important than another. To get the maximum buy-in we need to approach as many members as possible.

Solo sales people will approach each individually or all at once as a group. Group presentation is risky unless it is used to identify the specific needs and problems of the individuals. This can be too time-consuming and lead to boredom in the group.

A selling **team** (sales person, manager, director, etc.) can approach many different members almost simultaneously.

Wheels

While this is similar to the circle there is one significant difference – the person in the middle, normally someone with authority and control. Classically this can be a CEO in sole possession of many of the facts needed to make a decision. They may control the flow of information to other decision makers and influencers, and prevent sales people from meeting them. Those at the centre of the Wheel typically make decisions that suit their vested interests, or prevent decisions that threaten them.

Strategy: Who should we sell to? The same approach applies as with the Circle, but the central person is more significant than the others. They have the power to overrule others and have a vested interest as they control the flow of information. To get the maximum buy-in we need to approach as many members as possible.

Solo sales people will invariably try to approach the central person first or last.

The selling **team** approach will match our CEO to theirs, our production director to theirs, like position to like position.

Horizontal Chains

Members of a chain may have to report to seniors at different stages. Horizontal Chains can, for example, represent purchasing managers in four different companies within the same group, say, or four departmental managers in the same company. All have equal standing and status.

Strategy: Who should we sell to? To get the maximum buy-in we need to approach as many members as possible.

Solo sales people will approach each individually or all at once as a group. The danger of group presentation in the early stages is omnipresent here.

Team selling works well, once again matching like position to like position.

The Web

A complex and often disorganized group of individuals, with no obvious or clearly defined process, chain of 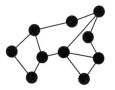 command or point of entry. Webs were historically common in local government and in local authorities such as public health services and hospital groups. Apathy and lethargy are the landmines in webs, because they lack leadership.

Strategy: Who should we sell to? The most complex of all, the web requires us to make multiple approaches, building Champions along the way and relying on them to help us create ripples of interest through the organization. This is by far the most time-intensive and frustrating.

Team selling is a real investment here because it's time intensive. The Approach Phase is a long one as playing the Web is a lot like being on a pinball machine, bounced repeatedly from pillar to post by contacts who will not acknowledge responsibility.

Therefore many companies rely on an extended **solo** approach.

THE SOLO APPROACH

As described in the examples above it is common for many organizations where the sales person is a solo selling resource and is expected to get out there and drag the bacon in kicking and screaming on their own. Where resource is limited this is understandable. However, in large-scale sales it is the kiss of death to gaining rapid and deep access. If the best possible chance of successful selling is gained through convincing as many decision makers and influencers as possible, the solo seller must do this either one contact at a time, or in group presentation. Group presentations do very little to help us accurately identify individual needs, problems and the cost of problems.

THE MULTIPLE OR TEAM SELLING APPROACH

This is much more like it! People buy from people whom they like or trust because they perceive them to be like them. So we put our CEO together with theirs and our sales director together with their commercial director, say. Meanwhile our sales person contacts others **and** manages the selling strategy. This reduces the time involved and increases the certainty of success. **But be careful: no sales person can afford to have colleagues (regardless of seniority) interacting with prospects without them personally having developed the right strategy-relevant skills** (see Chapter 4). In this way everybody involved is a **skilled** and managed part of the selling team.

Do you want the good news or the bad news? The good news is that genuinely we could leave the issue of the Decision-Making Unit right there. The geometric approach is reasonably thorough – it encourages us to target broad and deep – so we get better results using this than if we just engaged in traditional DMU targeting. The bad news is that Cascade Selling is not about being 'reasonably thorough'. It is about taking the shortest distance between two fixed points. The bad news is that it is more complex yet.

ARE YOU A DECISION MAKER?

A sales person gains access to a buying organization and starts asking questions to establish who the decision-making members of the DMU are; and then the sale starts unravelling like the Andrex puppy's toilet roll.

Danger! The moment you start asking questions with the word 'decision' in them, you're going to get trouble. Ask **anyone** in a buying organization about who makes decisions and in a high percentage of cases they'll tell you that they do, whether they do or not. Why? First, because everyone wants to feel good about themselves and this is as close as some get to their moment in the sun or Andy Warhol's 15 minutes of fame. And second, because they **know** (either intuitively or from bitter experience) that the minute a sales person smells someone more senior in the background, they will drop the now less important contact like a tofu sandwich.

The other danger is that asking for decision makers does not get you a list of people who are **not** decision makers. 'What the hell is he talking about? Why do I want to find people who are **not** decision-makers?' I hear you ask. Simple: because along the way, of course, you want to find out who the influencers are – those who have some say but no direct decision-making authority.

But in addition to this, and critically, you cannot afford to miss the Blocker. This person is also known as the Spanner Thrower or Wrench

Thrower. This individual can be anywhere in the organization and does not necessarily ping on a sweep of the decision-maker radar. Often they can be someone like an engineering supervisor, stores person or customer services supervisor, who may have no formal authority in a purchase but is a thought-leader whom others follow.

What a mess: decision makers and influencers, senior managers, middle managers and Blockers! You can't live with them and you threaten the sale without them. And all of this is compounded by the fact that asking for 'decision makers' will never get you a complete DMU.

THE MOST EFFECTIVE PENETRATION STRATEGY

The big question here is: *Who's the Daddy?* Who is it in a buying organization who has the ultimate power of veto? That is, the power to overrule all others, either positively or negatively. Who is it that can decide that the company is now going to use a new supplier whether others like it or not? This is the CEO, MD or Very Senior Person, right? So what is the risk if, for example, with an existing customer you do not have access to and a relationship with their CEO? Well, here's the simple truth: your business is vulnerable! It is not safe, protected, locked in or even stable. And if one of your competitors is targeting that individual, it is only a matter of time. Your revenues from that customer could vanish tomorrow like a ferret up a drainpipe and you will be powerless to stop it. If this is the case, what should you be doing right now with all of your high value existing customers? You've got it: developing action planning to gain access to their CEO, or as high up the organization as you can realistically get!

PROSPECT PENETRATION: THE CASCADE STRATEGY

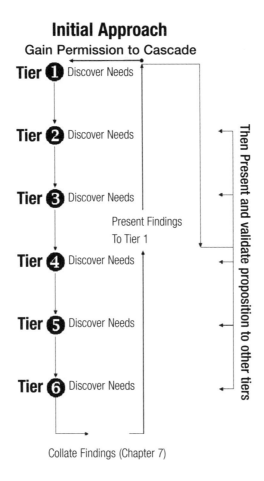

Collate Findings (Chapter 7)

We need a strategy that positions us for highly successful selling right from the start before we begin selling to anyone. To take a Cascade Approach we need to avoid as many of the pitfalls as possible and **aim for the optimum outcome**. For this we need a Cascade Strategy.

If you're a mere mortal and you're rolling a large boulder, which of the following is easier to do: is it easier to push the boulder uphill or to roll it down? It's always easier to roll it down thanks to gravity. The same thing applies in a prospect or customer company. Many organizations in a business-to-business environment operate in a vertically hierarchical way with different tiers of authority. CEO at the top, then directors below, followed by managers below that and so on.

Cascade Strategy targets the highest point of access into the prospect organization: CEO, MD, Very Senior Person or Tier 1. If you can gain access to the CEO, get their attention and interest and get them on your side, when you ask for their permission to **cascade** down through the organization to talk to all of the other **decision-relevant** people it is likely that they will **sponsor** you. When you're sponsored in this way everything happens so much faster. You go from contact to contact identifying problems, cost of problems, needs and the best potential proposition. And then you collect and present the findings back to the CEO, balancing for them the difference in scale between the problems and cost of them, and your proposition and its cost. Where the cost of the problem is greater than the cost of the proposition (which it invariably is if you have questioned your contacts thoroughly enough), **that** is called a compelling financial argument and CEOs **love** a compelling argument. Once you have presented it, however, they will not take it on trust, they will have their departmental managers validate it. (More of this to come.)

Selling through middle management decision makers or influencers can be as easy as running through treacle in snow shoes! Progress is ketchup-slow, direction is controlled by someone else, we do not have a clear picture of who the right people are, and our access to them is blocked by someone whose motivations at best are unclear and at worst are not to be trusted.

Starting at the top of the organization is like lighting a length of fuse wire with a blow torch.

THE CASCADE SEQUENCE

The sequence for initiating the Cascade Strategy looks like this:

1. Make an Initial Approach to the CEO (Chapter 4). Secure a face-to-face meeting or gain their authority to cascade to other relevant contacts in the business, and take some names.

2. If securing a face-to-face meeting keep the meeting brief... and then seek permission to cascade.

3. In either case – this is critical – secure an appointment to come back and present your findings. This will ideally be no longer than three weeks hence or they will forget who you are and so deselect your appointment.

4. When you approach each new contact, try using a Benefit Pitch (see Chapter 4) that interests them, not 'Your CEO says you have to talk to me' because you might create or trip over some explosive politics.

5. Every time you talk to a new contact ask them the question: 'Tell me: who else in the organization is affected by or is interested in this kind of conversation?' Identify the other relevant people to talk to each time you make a new contact. This will get you a cross-referenced and cross-checked list that is as close as you will ever get to the *full* list of people who are decision-relevant.

6. Work with each person to identify their operational/departmental problems. Focus on the ones that you can solve (see Chapter 5).

7. Identify the physical impact of the problems and their cost (see Chapter 5).

8. Present your overall findings back to the CEO (see Chapter 7).

9. Gain authority to present and prove your proposition to the other decision-relevant people in the business.

SOLO OR TEAM CASCADE

The Cascade Strategy can be accomplished by a solo sales person **if** they are talented enough to get in at the top level and get each of the subsequent contacts to reveal the right information. This method is designed to get the sales person **slingshot access** to as many of the right people as possible. So in real terms solo cascading can be highly effective.

If however a sales person is rejected at the top level they are faced with a number of choices:

1. They might have to try again but lower down. This can be the same net effect as starting your approach in the middle, so there are real downsides here.
2. However, they can always fall back on a team selling strategy so all is not yet lost. Perhaps someone else in the selling organization can retry the approach.
3. Additionally, they can try the top level again in a few weeks' time as it is unlikely that they will be remembered. The content upon which the second attempt is based will obviously need to be a significant improvement on the first.

The upside of a well-managed team sell is that we can have our CEO contact theirs and invite them to a commercial, sporting or social event, while we have a number of other colleagues initiate contact at other levels. Let's say that we decide on an approach to six different people all in the same week. Even with a percentage of failure we can still gain access to a good spread of decision-relevant people without being locked into one.

BUT WHAT ABOUT MY EXISTING LOCK-INS?

If you're reading this and thinking: 'But what about my existing business where I'm already locked in at middle management level and that person won't let me go above them?' You raise an interesting point. I have seen sales people try go over the heads of their contacts on literally hundreds of occasions and have never seen it work. But all is not lost. Try this: have your CEO contact theirs and invite him or her to lunch or for an HQ visit or perhaps a social event. Next time you speak to your contact (which might even be the same day if they are enough of a control freak) it's possible that they are going to be off their head and frothing at the mouth!

'WHAT THE HELL IS GOING ON? I TOLD YOU NOT TO GO OVER MY HEAD AND THE NEXT THING I KNOW, YOUR CEO IS HAVING LUNCH WITH MY CEO! WHAT ARE YOU PLAYING AT?'

Reply with equal vigour, volume and vehemence (mirroring): *'OH FOR CRYING OUT LOUD – I DON'T BELIEVE IT! MY CEO IS UNBELIEV- ABLE! I TRY KEEPING A HANDLE ON THE GUY BUT IT'S LIKE TRYING TO KEEP A LEASH ON A RHINO. HE'S ALWAYS CHARGING AROUND THE PLACE LIKE HE OWNS IT, RINGING CUSTOMERS AND INVITING THEM TO OUT LUNCH! IT'S OUTRAGEOUS!'*

So who will your contact think the bad guy is? It won't be you, will it? I hope your CEO likes lunching with high value prospects and customers!

IDENTIFYING FULL DECISION RELEVANCE USING THE DECISION- MAKING PROCESS (DMP)

If you're a sales person or sales organization with a hang-up on the DMU, abandon it now. Much more significant and productive is the DMP. Establishing the Decision-Making Process gets us into a lot less trouble. Sales people tend to make assumptions when thinking about decision-making power. They believe that formal decision-making bodies like committees, boards or management teams are the DMU. In doing so they fail to recognize that decisions are often made through less structured or clearly defined processes where any number of people – at any level – can influence a decision at different stages.

In order to identify the decision-relevant people that you need to talk to, ask about **the process**, and avoid the words 'decision' or 'decision making'. The form of words should be kept simple:

- What's the process that you go through here when you have this kind of conversation, Roger?
- Who gets involved?
- And who else?
- Anyone else?
- Tell me something, Patricia: who else do I need to talk to?
- Who else in the organization is affected by this kind of conversation?
- Who else in the organization is interested in this kind of conversation?
- Who else gets involved when you have these kinds of conversations?
- Who are the other interested parties here?
- Who would you recommend that I talk to, to gather the right information?
- Who else has a say here?

SILVERBACK

There are sales people who will say that actually getting to the top woman or man in very large organizations is virtually impossible so let's just aim lower down. I admit that there are times when you will have to do that, but it should never be used as an excuse for allowing our natural fear to get the better of us. And you'd be surprised at just how high you can reach. There are some great examples of this at the end of the next chapter.

I like to think that Cascade Selling, which has to be the Number One choice of Approach Strategy for highly successful sales people, is like the law of the jungle. If you penetrate anywhere below CEO or Very Senior Person level you will enter the jungle and will deal with the chimps and the monkeys: they're mischievous and they misbehave. They love to play games and pick fleas. They love to jibber-jabber and waste your time and none of them really has the power to call the shots – to drive the sale hot, straight and true right from its initiation. What you really want is to escape the jungle and deal with the one who is truly in charge. You want to deal with the Silverback, right? When the Silverback wants something he (or she) demands it, bangs his fists, the ground shakes and the others **jump!** In a Cascade Sale I'd much rather start by dealing with the Silverback and then move on to the monkeys.

This chapter answers the 'Who' of highly successful selling. From this point forwards the Cascade Selling methodology will focus on perfecting the Cascade Strategy at CEO level. While many sales people view this as being by far the most difficult level at which to make an approach it is probably the easiest **if** you do it right! So what we need next is the 'How'.

CHAPTER 4

STEP 4
HOW ARE
YOU GOING
TO GET THE
DOOR OPEN?

WHAT ARE YOU GOING TO SELL?

Let me ask you this: what are your major prospects interested in? By which I mean what will they buy from you? No, forget that. Let's try it a different way. Do you own a camera? Of course, you do. I don't mind what kind it is, digital or the traditional variety, just so long as it takes pictures. Let me ask you this. What is it that you buy when you buy a camera?

Ask this of a group of ten different people and you'll get ten different answers: brand: reliability, association, trustworthiness, etc. Feature functionality: it has ten megapixels and autofocus. It's cheap: I keep losing them so I only want to spend five pounds. A photograph! And so on.

If you're lucky, some bright spark will pipe up with 'Memories' (hopefully without breaking into song). Now this is interesting because it takes us a step beyond the normal (traditional selling) product-based answers. If you consider the old adage that when you buy a power drill what you're actually buying is a ten-millimetre-diameter hole you'll get a feeling for where we're going with this.

What is it that you buy when you buy a camera? Yes, you buy all the product feature-functionality, and you get a picture **and** a method of capturing and archiving memories to be accessed any time you please.

The physical or product part of this is the photograph. But even if it's a beautiful eye-candy shot of a desert island it doesn't end there. There is so much more to a piece of celluloid than meets the eye. If you're a little bit clever the edges of a photograph are elastic: you can stretch them and climb into it. You can go back to a place and time of your choosing. If you're quite clever you can **hear** the waves gently lapping against the shore. You can **smell** the scent of lilies on the breeze. You can **hear** the trade winds gently clacking through the palm fronds. If you're **very** clever you can **feel** the sand between your toes!

Tomorrow you decide to resign from your job and fulfil a life's ambition. You've always wanted to go into business for yourself; you've always wanted your own camera shop. And while you're thinking about things like a name for the business and a strap line, two alternatives pop into your head: either (and your name for the sake of this example will need to be either Barney or Barbara) Barney's (or Barbara's) Bargain Basement Box Brownie Business – We stack 'em high and sell 'em cheap. Or: Sand Between the Toes.

Which of these images do you think is more likely to sell? Which of these do you think is the sexier selling message? As much as I like the answer that the second one is sexier, the reality is that it depends on whether the buyer's Interface Style is logical or emotional.

Now let's return to the original question. What are your major prospects interested in? By which I mean: what will they buy from you? The answer is that it depends on what 'Sand Between the Toes' is for them individually. In Cascade Selling this is referred to as the **end-zone benefit**: the largest possible believable or relevant benefit in the chain.

THE END ZONE – TOUCHDOWN!

Wouldn't it be nice if we could predict **certainty of sale** based on what happens in the selling process? Wouldn't it be nice if we could be sure of a sales win because the customer can't or doesn't want to say 'No' to us?

If only we could get inside the heads of the people that we sell to and **know** what their end zone benefits really are! Granted, we know that one major benefit is the critical factor of chemistry – the Interface Skills – and we already know that we can have a major impact in that area. But that's only half the story. It's the commercial drivers that are far less clear in so many sales situations. The prospect or customer will tell you (if they don't tell you to 'Get Lost' first) what they want. But, of course, they will be happy to dictate their wants to any sales person – so that's differentiation getting on the Big Yellow Bus; wave goodbye to the bus! It's their **needs** that are the critical bit. In truth, unless we are skilful enough to uncover the end-zone benefits that will turn them on, their Key Purchase Criteria, what chance do we have of building **any** certainty into the sale?

LOVE THOSE FUNKY RESEARCHERS

It would be fair to say that if we really wanted to find out where the purchasing hooks lie, and let's complicate this by *identifying them at every level of decision-relevant authority*, it would take a good deal of time and your organization's resources to do it, especially with any degree of accuracy. Which makes it a non-starter, right? Also, forget paying a market research company to do it because with information this sensitive it's unlikely that they will get the most honest and accurate feedback. And let's face it, the cost would probably be prohibitive.

So let's pause for a moment. How on earth would you realistically go about finding out the Key Purchase Criteria (the key decision-making factors) of the people that you want to sell to? Well, do a little dance, make a little love, and get down tonight because here's something we prepared earlier!

I have worked with the Chartered Institute of Marketing for 10 years as a course director. The Institute is split into a number of areas: two of which include Training and Membership. At last count there was something like a 48,000 worldwide membership. You become a member for a multitude of reasons but one of the main ones is that members want to be associated with a body that values their voice when it comes to issues surrounding the marketing (and sales) professions. So like all good marketers the Institute regularly surveys its membership base and asks for comment and feedback on contentious issues of the moment.

SOLID GOLD

Have you ever sent out a customer survey, or even the dreaded customer satisfaction survey? You know what it's like: for months you design the thing (nobody ever agrees on what it should look like or contain), and then you incur the cost of getting 10,000 printed, stuffed and posted... and after all that effort you get three replies. Two are return-to-sender because they were sent to the wrong address. And the third is dissatisfied, thinks your service sucks, and wants a price reduction! But The Chartered Institute of Marketing members **want** to be surveyed; they want to be asked for their point of view. As a result the Institute frequently gets a significantly higher than average reply rate. One of the surveys undertaken by them about four years ago involved members in the top 100 companies in the UK. These members were asked to list their Key Purchase Criteria upon which they select new key suppliers or test existing suppliers against others in the market. As usual a very high percentage of those polled responded; the responses were collated into a refined list, and broken down into tiers by the hierarchical level of respondents. The list and its contents are made from *solid gold* if you want your prospect or customer sales approaches to strike oil fast. It is the formal identification of Sand Between the Toes.

SIX TIERS OF BUYING WINS

Tier and Position	Broad KPC	Detailed KPC
1. Top Management	Financial improvement	– Long-term security
		– Image
		– Competitive edge
		– Return on Investment/ cash flow
	Operational improvement	– Reduce costs/labour, materials, energy
		– Reduce investments
		– Consolidate functions/ streamline processes
		– Competitive advantage
	People improvement	– Management performance and development
		– Workforce performance and attitudes
2. Financial Management	Yield and increased efficiencies	– Rate of Return
		– Verifiable Payback/ ROI
		– Expenditure gearing
		– Calculations to MD
		– Efficiency factors

3. Middle Management	Solving problems	– Improving operations
		– Change easy to understand
		– Ease of implementation/ no disruption
		– Smooth transition from old to new
		– Improvements: People/ Productivity/ Manufacturing/ QC/ Inventory Control/Sales, etc.
4. Purchasing	Price/ concessions	– Discounts
		– Retrospective bonuses
		– Credit
		– Fixed pricing
		– Contractual issues
5. Technical Specialists	Capability	– Specifications
		– State-of-the-art
		– Industry leading/ Showcase
		– Operational performance
		– Reliability and Longevity
6. Operator or User (Staff Level)	Personal performance	– Level of personal service
		– Personal skills improvement
		– Enhanced job performance
		– Enhanced personal image
		– Enhanced career progression
		– Enhanced market value/ future salary

The first column is a prospect's Tier (rank) and job position, the second column their broad Key Purchase Criteria (area of interest) and the third column defines some of the more tactical KPCs that are positively impacted when the broad appeal is fulfilled.

Sales people can fall into the trap of selling what they *think* the buying contact wants, **not** what they actually need. Before we pitch anything we need to anticipate and identify the real purchase criteria behind their buying decision – the factors that are essential in getting any decision-relevant individual to say 'Yes' based on the commercial benefit that we might be able to provide.

Tier 1: Top Management

This refers to CEOs and MDs. Ask yourself the question: what are the primary responsibilities of someone in that position? What's important to them? What are their benchmarks, points of measurement, key performance indicators? If you had to define a day in the life of a CEO, what would be on their task list?

> **Broad appeal** is summarized as the three key tasks for which they're responsible: financial, operational and people improvement. Why are these things important? First, Tier 1s are employed to manage and grow the financial performance of the business: turnover and profit. Operational improvement is a key contributor to this. If you improve the operation you reduce costs and increase output. Simply put, more is produced for less. People improvement is another key contributor. If you improve the people then productivity should also increase. They work more effectively and efficiently, once again producing more for less. Second, some people would also point out that Tier 1s earn their bonus based on financial improvement.

Detailed appeal is the physical area in which the improvement is made; a key and more localized area of benefit.

Tier 2: Financial Management

Very often sales people believe that the financial director is the ultimate decision maker, blind to the reporting relationship that they have with the Tier 1 and the financial resource or legwork that they provide. FDs should often be seen as one rung below the top tier and as a conduit that needs winning so that they will present the right argument in the right way. To do that, as with the others, you have to understand both their specialized thinking and their vocabulary. In simple terms the information that you give them needs to be specific to their company and situation, not generic, and should make their calculations as easy and logical as possible. In other words, they need to be able to understand where or whom the maths comes from and it should be verifiable. They need to be able to check it at source. After that their interest lies in the Rate of Return from increases in efficiency say, reductions in the cost base, how the acquisition fits in with their gearing (finance instead of capital acquisition, for example), and ultimately what they get back for their investment: Return on Investment (ROI) or yield.

Tier 3: Middle Management

This relates to managers of departments. Classically these are the people caught between a rock and a hard place. They are the 100 per cent pure beef burger in the business quarter-pounder. The sesame seed bun above them is top management, below them the staff. Everyone tries taking a bite out of middle management. They are under constant and daily pressure from two different directions. Top management demands that strategies are fulfilled, efficiencies, quotas and budgets are met. Members of staff demand the things that are important to them: salary increases, promotions, extra time-off, incentives and rewards. Middle managers spend the majority of their existence dealing with other people's demands and problems, and then they have their own job to do. Solve or remove a problem, make their life easier and you will become a highly valued asset.

Tier 4: Purchasing

This is a clear-cut case. One of the primary functions of purchasing is to reduce the cost of the company's purchases. Where purchasing is instructed to strike the best deal with one of a choice of potential suppliers, our margin battle is potentially lost, and the balance of power rests firmly with the purchaser. When, however, we have employed a Cascade Strategy and at all levels of the company the decision relevant have told purchasing to order from one supplier, us, the balance of power shifts firmly to the seller. And we'll have fun, fun, fun 'till Daddy takes the T'Bird away'.

Tier 5: Technical Specialists

This is also clear-cut. They are tasked with ensuring that the company makes the best technical and technology decisions, acquiring systems that fit with the organization, and from which the specialists can milk maximum efficiency, effectiveness and therefore output. What they care about is the technical capability of the product and how advanced it is.

Tier 6: Operators or Users

Members of staff are the practitioners. Anything that will help them to do their job more easily, and that will reflect well on them from a capability, skills development and reward perspective, will always be welcome.

Granted, this is by no means exhaustive, and does not account for more recent topical issues of the day e.g. compliance, health and safety, etc. However as a baseline it gives us something really tangible to work with. The only question is – how do we put it to best use?

NEXT STEP

It is critical that sales people identify which of the Buying Wins they can fulfil and then set about convincing prospects and customers of their expertise in these areas. It is always useful to question the value that each Buying Win actually represents before you demonstrate fulfilment of it, and to identify others that might not be on the list above.

If your products or services fulfil the Buying Wins of any or all of the tiers, you need to ensure that with a prospect you demonstrate this as part of your proposition. With a customer you need to ensure that you are providing for and reinforcing their Buying Wins.

There are many methods of doing this dependent on the tier and the win. For instance, with a Tier 6, 'Level of personal service' might be a telephone and email helpline and a visit from your service engineer quarterly. With a Tier 1, 'Return on Investment' might be providing them with a simple quarterly ROI forecast. If this isn't your area of expertise, ask your financial director for a demonstration, or look at Chapter 7 for something equally powerful.

The real value in this information comes when embarking on what I think is the most difficult phase of selling. This is the Initial Approach: picking up the telephone on a cold call and grabbing the attention and interest of the prospect for long enough for you to get that all-important first commitment, for example an Initial Appointment.

Buying Wins are fantastic as the basis of Initial Approach technique, especially considering the limited amount of time before a call-recipient verbalizes their first (and often call-terminating) objection.

CARE TO TAKE A RIDE?

So maybe we know what lights the fire of six different tiers of decision-relevant authority in business but what the hell do we do with it now? For this next step we take a valuable page from the American Book of Business and adapt it a little for our needs. In order to get the most from the Initial Approach we have to understand the *concept* of the Elevator (Lift) Pitch. This tool has had its fair share of good and bad press over the years, mainly because of how it has been used and abused.

Used effectively it goes like this: you're at a networking event and you're stalking (in a good way, obviously) the CEO of a major prospect that you've been trying to break into for months. He heads for the lift (or elevator) to attend a session on the second floor. You step into the lift with 20 seconds before the doors open again. Will what you have to say inspire him to give you his business card or will it cause him to yawn? Put another way: when you pitch, is it sexy enough to get the recipient to show you some genuine attention and interest and give you a meaningful commitment? To make your pitch sexy, not only do you have to focus on distilling everything you do down to the main benefit ('sand between the toes') but you also have to deliver it in a timescale that doesn't remove the recipient's will to live! Get this wrong and once again you will operate frustratingly high rejection rates!

LIFE CHANGING?

But it's not as easy as it sounds, is it? The message needs to be short, powerful and if you're dealing with Tier 1 **Drivers** it needs to be **to the point!**

And the point has nothing whatsoever to do with products, services, features or brand! It has got to be a key benefit that you can deliver that is **totally** relevant to the tier of the person whom you are approaching, **and** in a manner designed to grab their attention and interest.

This is the moment that we've all been waiting for, where you have the opportunity to positively change your life. Don't get me wrong – I'm not suggesting that you are about to have a deeply spiritual epiphany – but this is an opportunity for you to *change your tactics and revolutionize your sales results for ever.*

BENCHMARK

If you're a sales leader, you're going to love this. Sit in with your sales people on their telephone cold calls and note down their Approach Dialogue. This is the form of words that they use right at the start of the call when they speak to the target prospect for the very first time. Or if you're a sales person, write down the words that you normally use. You know the kind of thing:

> Good morning, Mr Smith. My name is John Harward from a company called Crank Handle Limited. The reason for my call to you this morning, is to introduce myself and my company and see if there is the possibility that we might have something in common. As a company we manufacture and supply a full range of crank handles used specifically in the production area of your business, with full after-sales care and engineering support. I wondered if you might be interested in getting together for five minutes to discuss our crank handles and how they might be useful to you.

Now this may be typical or atypical of the words that you hear or use. That part doesn't matter; it's important to record *whatever* is used as a benchmark.

For the record, though, as a sales assessor I have heard this style, method, duration and content more times than a cuckoo has popped out of a wooden box.

YOU NEVER GET A SECOND CHANCE...

How long do you think you've got in which to get your message across on a telephone cold call before the prospect says, 'Get lost, I'm not interested'? Think about it: prospects receive countless cold calls on a daily basis. Many from sales people who are about as interesting as a tax inspection. Many of these sales people use Trigger Phrases; and they don't trigger positive things like 'Oh thank goodness you called!' They trigger **negative** impacts, emotions and responses. So how would you feel if you were the call recipient or the target prospect? **How long** would you give the sales person before you consciously or subconsciously made a negative decision and started putting out objections like a muck spreader in autumn? Write down the number that you think, measured in seconds (*pause for not-so-frantic scribbling*).

The answer to this comes from a study (reported in the *Sunday Times*) that was conducted into how quickly professional job interviewers make a hire or not hire decision when interviewing job applicants. Thousands of interviews were observed and the conclusions were fascinating. Apart from the timescale that was identified, it noted that: 'Within the confines of the scant opening pleasantries, the hiring decision is usually made. Favourable decisions can be reversed by the candidate's subsequent answers, but a negative impression cannot.'

Once you have made a negative impression the interviewer will consciously or subconsciously make an irreversible decision. If you screw it up 'Within the confines of the scant opening pleasantries' it's game over! You won't get the job! If you look or smell wrong, use the wrong handshake, don't seem confident enough, seem **too** confident, have bad breath, are dressed unsuitably, have a Mohican hairstyle when something more conservative is called for – any or all of these things are sufficient to cost you the job.

On the other hand, imagine this: you are conducting the best job interview of your life. The candidate is **perfect**. They look great, sound great, fit the team dynamic superbly and have got exactly the right experience. They couldn't be any better. They're so good, in fact, that you're wondering if it's too early to propose. Normally you would conduct three separate interviews but the hell with that. You're going to offer them the job now. But as you glance at your watch you notice that you've only been interviewing for 25 minutes. You can't offer them the job after **only 25** minutes. That would look desperate. So you decide to pad the interview out with a couple of personal questions:

'So Greg, what do you do when you're not working? What do you do in your spare time?' you ask, oozing genuine interest.

Greg replies: 'Well I do enjoy dressing up, and I have a fabulous collection of rubber chickens.'

Favourable decisions can be reversed by the candidate's subsequent answers, in the same way that any sales person can talk a prospect out of saying 'Yes'.

We are able to put the findings from this study to good use because job interviewing and selling as professional activities are remarkably similar. Trying to convince a complete stranger that you're worth the money, the benefit package and all that responsibility is probably the biggest job of selling that you will ever do – apart from, maybe, convincing some poor fool to marry you! If we translate the the *Sunday Times* quotation ('Within the confines…') into a sales environment it means that if you get your approach wrong and create any kind of negative impression the sale will get on the Big Yellow Bus! Wave goodbye to the bus.

So, I asked you to write down how long (measured in seconds) you would give a sales person before you objected. In selling, you are first allowed to

'Establish your Bona Fides': 'Hi, my name is John Harward from Crank Handle Limited' and the clock will **not** start ticking. It starts the moment you begin speaking again. **Then** you have 34 seconds in which to positively **get** their attention. Oh, I'm sorry. I made a mistake: you have **three to four seconds** in which to get their attention. **That's four seconds.** In a face-to-face job interview this is about the duration of time it takes for the candidate to knock, enter the room, greet the interviewer and maybe get as far as shaking them by the hand. In a massively high percentage of cases the study noted that the professional job interviewer had already made their decision by this point, having judged the candidate's book by its cover and gone on first impressions. You see? You never get a second chance to make the *right* first impression.

So let's try our earlier Approach Dialogue shall we?

Good morning, Mr Smith. My name is John Harward from a company called Crank Handle Limited.

[Now the clock starts ticking.]

The reason for my call to you this morning, is to introduce myself and my company and see if there is the possibility that we might have something in common. As a company we manufacture and supply a full range of crank handles used specifically in the production area of your business, with full after-sales care and engineering support. I wondered if you might be interested in getting together for five minutes to discuss our crank handles and how they might be useful to you.'

OOH – 26 seconds!

OBJECTION CITY

If you ever get to the end of this dialogue without them interrupting I will personally **guarantee Objection City**: I'm too busy/ I'm in a meeting (so why did you answer the phone?)/ We're very happy with our current supplier/ I'm not interested/ Put something in the post/ Give us a call back after Christmas (which in February is quite worrying)/No, we don't need any of that, and so on… And a sales person realizes this subconsciously after about four seconds, which is why they speed up their pitch and finish the dialogue at the same speed as Usain Bolt at the Olympics, and without drawing breath!

Additionally, the unintentional or unplanned use of **Trigger Phrases (in bold)** will cause the prospect to see red in some form:

> Good morning, **Mr Smith. My name is** John Harward **from a company** called Crank Handle **Limited. The reason for my call to you this morning, is to introduce myself and my company** and **see if there is the possibility** that **we might have something in common. As a company** we manufacture and supply a full range of crank handles used specifically in the production area of your business, with full after-sales care and engineering support. I **wondered if you might** be interested in **getting together for five minutes** to discuss our crank handles and how they **might be** useful to you.

'DON'T WASTE MY TIME'

Why are the bold words Trigger Phrases?

'Good morning, **Mr Smith**'. If you use this form of address *in the UK*, you are automatically subservient. What we wish to create here is the perception of *mutuality*: the prospect is an important Tier 1 CEO, and you are important too. The only person that a Tier 1 is interested in talking to if birds of a feather flock together is another CEO or someone who sounds *as important*. Tier 1s hate sales people because they never get to the point; they just waste the Tier 1's time, as many of the other Trigger Phrases will demonstrate. Of course, the sales person's perception is that if they use the Tier 1's first name they are being too forward too early. In 25 years of selling I've been corrected by Tier 1s one time in a thousand. Be advised, however, that there are some countries (Germany, for example) where the use of the full name and title are still mandatory, so cultural factors are left to your discretion.

'**My name is** (time wasting) John Harward **from a company called** (time wasting again) Crank Handle **Limited** (<u>sales people</u> tell you in their approach that their business is Limited: *business people* do not. Which do you want to be seen as? And at this stage Limited Liability is irrelevant, time wasting).'

'**The reason for my call to you this morning** (time wasting) **is to introduce myself and my company** (time wasting) and **see if there is the possibility** (time wasting and Tier 1s do not deal in possibilities, they are interested only in certainties) that **we might have something in common** (time wasting: too vague – be more specific). **As a company** [no, really? A company you say? Time wasting]… **I wondered if you might** ('might' isn't a certainty) be interested in **getting together for five minutes (Gotcha!** This is a famous sales lie: Tier 1s can smell it at a thousand metres. What can you realistically achieve in five minutes? What you want is an hour but aren't *confident* enough about the benefits that you can offer to ask for it honestly! They believe that you will end up wasting their time) to discuss our crank handles and how they **might be** (uncertainty and time wasting again) useful to you.'

Additionally there are all the old classic Trigger Phrases! Whenever a sales person initiates an approach the clock is ticking and *the wrong word or phrase* can spell doom, triggering objections and resistance from the listener. Here are some of the worst:

– How are you?

– I was hoping I could take five minutes of your time?

– I just wanted five minutes…

– Can you talk?

– Can you spare me a moment?

– Is it convenient to talk?

– Have you heard of us?

– I don't know if you've heard of us?

– I'd like to talk to you about…

– Can I ask you a few questions?

SMOOTH

As the establishing of bona fides above includes Trigger Phrases it is highly likely that the sales person would experience **very** early objections. If you remove the Trigger Phrases, and smooth the mismatched grammar that naturally results, you are left with something like this:

(Good morning, Roger. I'm John Harward from Crankhandle.)
We manufacture and supply a full range of crank handles used specifically in the production area of your business, with full after-sales care and engineering support. I'd like to arrange a meeting to discuss our products (avoids repetition) and how they can be useful to you.

OOH: 14 seconds!

Wow! We've almost halved the duration of the Approach Dialogue. Do you like it? No, I'm not too keen on it either. Not only is it still too long and a bit boring, but it also breaks two BIG sales rules: it is feature-oriented (not benefit) **and** it doesn't finish in an open question (Golden Sales Rule no, 749: sales people should never make statements in isolation; everything they say should finish in a question or a close).

JIM'LL FIX IT

Task 1: Shorten it – this will iron itself out when we get to the pitch below.

Task 2: Present **benefits not features** and finish with an Open Question. Select the **Buying Win** (benefit) relevant to the job level of the person to whom you're going to pitch. In our case this will be a Tier 1.

Then we need to smarten up the content of that 14-second Approach Dialogue. To do this without taking the rest of our lives, we would benefit from a technique; something tried and tested. You would think there are dozens of techniques out there with which to get this particular job done. Not so; in all my time as a trainer I have only come across **one** that is any good. It's called:

THE BENEFIT PITCH

The idea of using a 'Pitch' is not a new one. *Genuinely* brand new inventions in sales are rare. There are many types of introduction out there, all of which I think are a pitch of one sort or another. Some of the classic well-known pitches include the initial benefit statement and the opening benefit statement, both of which are decades old.

Having heard many examples of both kinds of statement over the years, however, they both tend to have one thing in common. The alleged 'benefit' used is always either a feature (figure that one out) or an advantage so close to the original feature that it sounds like a feature. Also, no attention is paid to the time critical nature of the approach, with sales people rambling on for upwards of 30 seconds. And we now know how painful that is!

In Cascade Selling we seek to create a finely tuned approach: we step up to the plate with not any old bat. We step up with a Louisville Slugger. The benefit that we use is so appealing that the ball's heading for the stratosphere!

There are three variations of the Benefit Pitch, and they do what they say on the tin. They initiate the dialogue with a highly attractive Buying Win. They are also constructed to maximize attention and interest from the recipient in a *minimalist* period of time. Forget three to four seconds here: there is no way that you are going to get anything useful across in four seconds. Ignoring the bona fides as usual, it would be this:

'We manufacture and supply a full range of crank handles used specifically...'

Four seconds

You see? No go. So we have to sensibly reduce the 14 seconds whilst gaining *sufficient* positive attention to move us to the next step in the Progression, which is Needs Discovery. This takes place around conversation. We ask the questions and they answer them. This is, of course, in pursuit of a qualified appointment, say, or commitment to the next stage in the process, whatever you want that to be.

The techniques that you are about to see are constructed specifically to meet all of the challenges that we have discussed so far. You can use them undiluted, or you can evolve them for yourself, but be careful. The more you change them away from their original construction, the more likely you are to break them, and reduce their potentially positive impact. You can also take it for granted that each example will have been initiated after establishing your bona fides.

The Name Dropper Pitch: the name that you drop might be someone whom they know personally, someone in their network, supply or indeed customer chain. Or perhaps you supply a company whom you know *they* will know. Be careful with using their competitors though as this will often be rejected by them as a Fear Close. A last resort is to use a household name. Using the Name Dropper requires some research.

'Roger – we've been working with Crackerjack over the past six months to help them **substantially reduce their operating costs**. Tell me something: how important is overhead reduction in your business currently?'

Nine seconds

- This technique is designed and constructed specifically to gain attention and interest.
- The first name is used (in the UK and some other countries) to breed mutuality.
- We get to the reference fast. Name dropping does not guarantee that Roger will welcome us *all the way in* with open arms but it does buy some credibility and he also knows he can check up on us with Crackerjack.
- Six months has to be a real time period, but whatever the timescale (if longer than a few months obviously) it implies that we are an entrenched supplier of value.
- The Buying Win comes straight from the Six Tiers table and has to be one that you are capable of delivering by virtue of the benefits that your products and services provide.
- 'Tell me something' is an imperative. You can also use 'Tell me'. We go into real detail on this technique in the next chapter but for now the reason that they are specifically used when pitching is that this is a very com-

manding method of raising attention in the second half of the statement.
- The question that follows this is open to get an informational response. This is discussed in greater detail in Chapter 5.
- The benefit is rephrased in the second half to avoid irritating repetition.
- The next two pitches that you will see follow the same structure.

In my experience networking and name dropping are the most powerful ways of breaking into new business. The fuel for this technique is in ensuring that your contact database is stuffed full of as many useful contacts as possible. We cover this in more detail in Chapter 8. But you won't *always* have someone that you can name drop, so we need an alternative.

The Market Intelligence Pitch: this is based on a *reliable* piece of market intelligence. Let's say that a newly elected President of the United States has announced the immediate imposition of import levies on foreign steel, killing the competitive edge of steel producers outside the United States wishing to sell in. You contact the Tier 1 of a major steel company whose main export market is America. You are from a process re-engineering business. You have heard from contacts in the industry, or from the national news, that because of such dramatic events major redundancies are anticipated in the next few weeks.

'Roger – we understand with the recent news coming out of the US that **regaining competitive edge** is a real focal point for the industry. Tell me: to what degree is market consolidation top of your list of priorities right now?'

11 seconds

Be honest – if you were the person receiving that call you couldn't help but be interested. Hot news is really juicy: we strike while the iron is white hot. This is why recruitment consultants ring you as soon as you place a job advert, because they *know* that you're in the market and as a result they'll get your attention at the very least. In my view the Market Intelligence Pitch is the second most powerful of the three techniques. Regrettably, a great piece of accurate intelligence won't always be available so we fall back on the third technique.

The Generic Pitch: this is the man or woman for all seasons. If you can't use the other two, ultimately you have to fall back on something less topical, and as a result, I believe, less powerful. This one is targeted at large companies in major conurbations where the cost per square foot or metre of office space is a constant thorn in their side:

> 'Roger – we're being driven by our clients currently to help them **maximize the Return on Investment** on every square inch of administrative space. Tell me something: how important is leveraging this kind of asset to you in your business right now?'

11 seconds

While it is definitely more generalized and less topical than the other two, I think it is infinitely more refined and interesting than the Crank Handle introduction, don't you?

MORE? YOU WANT MORE?

Here are some additional examples of Benefit Pitches:

> 'We're working with local businesses at the moment to help them drive down the cost of fleet maintenance. Tell me Roger, how important are cost savings in your fleet at the moment?'

'Patricia, we've been working with Crackhammer over the past nine months to identify key areas where they can reduce operational costs. Tell me something: how important is overhead reduction in your company right now?'

'We've been playing a major part in helping Merlin Telecoms to boost the sales of their new Premium Service. Tell me Barney: how important is competitive edge to you in your market currently?'

'I understand that with the recent slowdown in the textiles industry it's become more important than ever to ensure that staff are 100 per cent effective. Tell me something Angelina: how important is maximizing productivity in your business currently?'

'Amanda, we specialize in working with our customers to ensure that the manufacturing process is as cost effective as possible. Tell me: how important is operational cost control to you at the moment?'

'Jean-Paul, we specialize in working with our clients to help them dramatically increase revenues. Tell me something: how important is sales growth in your business right now?'

And an example of one that could be used with an existing customer operation:

'Last year we saved your business 300k on one mechanical issue. We saved Fast and Loose Powerboats 1.2m on the same type of issues. How interested would you be in this kind of saving?'

THE ACID TEST

These techniques are being used today by thousands of successful sales people. But before I allowed any of my sales training delegates to use the latest version for the first time, I tested them on a selection of *difficult* CEOs. The most noteworthy CEO's name I will not repeat but his nickname is Frostie, and he is the former CEO of one of the largest drinks companies in the world. But more recently Frostie has been found sitting in his office overlooking Kowloon Bay in Hong Kong as CEO of a different organization. He is right at the upper end of the scale that defines Tier 1 Driver CEOs. For entertainment and to keep his teeth sharp he always accepts inbound calls from sales people. I have sat there in his office and watched him devour cold calling sales people in less than ten seconds! And without even belching afterwards! He's a successful, loud, witheringly direct and highly dominating individual whose *natural* style is Expressive so socially he's one of the most entertaining men on earth!

I tried a standard Tier 1 Name Dropper Pitch on him, after briefing him that he would recognize 'Crackerjack': 'Frostie – we've been working with Crackerjack over the past six months to help them **substantially reduce their operating costs.** Tell me something: how important is overhead reduction in your business currently?'

I cringed, covered my jugular and waited for the response. He thought for just a moment and then emitted a loud expletive: 'Bugg*r!'

Not the most helpful of responses, I thought, but at least he didn't say 'Bugg*r off!' so I suppose I should have been thankful for small mercies. He continued: 'About time one of you people got to the point! What are you selling?'

Being put on the spot like this is enough to give any sales person a mild cardiac arrest, but *hurrah for Frostie!* He gave me a buying signal. If you get to an interesting point fast with a Tier 1 personality, and know exactly what to do after the buying signal, the sales call *won't* join the *Titanic*!

THE VODKA AND TONIC TEST

A reassuring piece of feedback on this technique came from a sales person that I trained even more recently. He works for the Licensed Products Division of a large and well-known jewellery brand. I ran a training course for the sales team who sell to jewellery stores and chains. We ran two one-day sessions, one month apart. First they learned some skills and then they had the chance to go away and use them for a month before we developed the next set of complementary skills. On the first day we covered Benefit Pitches, building and practising techniques specific to jewellery store owners (Tier 1) for use on face-to-face cold calls.

A month later we all got together again and I started the day by asking how everybody had fared with the use of their pitches. One of the delegates piped right up. He said: 'Greg. I thought that session that you ran on pitching was rubbish. I thought it was a complete waste of time.'

'Which is nice', I thought.

He continued: 'So the first call I made after the course was a face-to-face cold call on a jewellery store owner in my home town. I went in and just slipped into my standard introduction, and because we'd practised watching how they react, I did. I saw all the interest drain out of the guy like air leaving the Michelin Man. I panicked! I thought "Oh crikey, what the hell do I do now?" But because we had done so many pitch rehearsals in the training room I recovered my wits a bit and delivered one of the benefit pitches that I had rehearsed. And do you know what? I saw the interest come back into the guy with a rush. The Michelin Man reinflated like someone had stuck an airline into him!'

THE TEQUILA, VODKA AND RED BULL TEST

I was working with a group very recently, and we were engaged in developing strategy and tactics for them to embark successfully on Big Account Selling. This is their name for the pursuit of high volume new business via a Tier 1 Approach and Cascade Strategy. We had targeted the relevant businesses, identified the Tier 1 personalities and formed suitable Benefit Pitches. When the time arrived to pick up the phones and make the calls it became obvious that many of the sales people felt a little nervous and that Tier 1 approaches were beyond their experience curve and outside their comfort zone. So in order to help them break through the fear threshold we did a little rehearsing and then I set a challenge, with a bottle of champagne for the winner. That morning I had been reading a business newspaper in their reception area. On the front page was an article about a Global Tier 1 of a business group with a turnover of €22 billion. Splashed across the front of the paper was a colour photo of the man. He looked cool, calm and professional. He had a gaze that could slice through armour plating – and you knew that he had probably vaporized more sales people with that gaze than Darth Vader. You know what's coming, don't you? Getting nervous yet?

Given the scale of the challenge I should have offered a *lifetime* supply of champagne. I tasked each individual in the group to telephone this CEO and deliver a Benefit Pitch and find out if they could gain access to the 400+ companies in the group with a view to selling to each of them, having gained sponsorship from the Tier 1. Let's face it: what on earth was there to lose here? This guy was likely to be better screened than the Pope so the odds of actually getting through to him were about the same as staying upright during a round of 'friendly' sparring with Mike Tyson. Also, he was outside of their typical sales circles so even if they completely screwed the pooch – who cared? There was no downside. Unbelievably, his telephone number popped right out of a Google search. And so I left them to decide who was going to call him first and finished the session wondering what would happen next?

Two days later I received a call from one of the delegates. Our conversation went like this:

Hans: Greg. I did it. I called the Tier 1. And I got through!

Greg: Wow! That's fantastic – what happened?

Hans: I was on the phone for two-and-a-half minutes.

Greg: What did you say to him?

Hans: I used a Benefit Pitch that talked about being able to dramatically reduce his operating costs.

Greg: What did he say?

Hans: He said he has somebody that deals with all of that for him. I was so nervous that I couldn't think of what to say next, and I could hear my voice trembling...

That call was probably the most difficult that Hans will ever make and what a fantastic result! He got through to a €22 billion – *billion* – intimidating looking Tier 1, and engaged in 150 seconds of conversation. Yes he was nervous and no the approach didn't lead to anything on that call. BUT, he broke through the fear threshold and handled himself. Next time, a little extra preparation will pay dividends. And calling any terrestrial CEO now should be no more intimidating than chatting with his sister Gertrude over a litre of schnapps.

RIGHT NOW

'Right now', 'currently' or similar phrases used at the end of the pitch are more important than you might think. Using a 'right now' reference causes the Tier 1 to answer whether your pitch topic is hot and interesting **now**. If you leave it open without 'right now' they will say or think, 'Well, of course, it's really important'. But it might not be the thing that's burning a hole in their soul, right up at the top of today's priority list, instead of mere generic appeal. So the approach *might* continue for a few minutes longer but sometime thereafter the objections will start, and the call will get on the Big Yellow Bus.

BULLSEYE BENEFIT PITCHES

You can use textbook Benefit Pitches. Most sales people using this system use them undiluted as they fit a high percentage of Tier 1 personalities. But the best Benefit Pitches are based on a little research that tells us how important the issue is right now. This form of ground truth (*what's really* happening on the ground) helps us to seize the moment. But be careful what you believe. If a company publishes a press release that says: 'This quarter we are focusing on promoting social conscience and environmental responsibility' then as an experienced sales professional I am **not** going to approach them with the following Benefit Pitch:

> 'Roger, we've been working with Stompwijk Industries over the past nine months to help them uplift their environmental responsibility. Tell me something: how important is the Green Agenda in your business right now?'

The reason that I am not going to take this alleged focus at face value is because there is a world of difference between what companies pump out as PR and the ground truth. The question I am more interested in is 'Why' they are interested in these things. I believe that the best research in this kind of situation is done at ground level, with both staff and departmental managers. Let's say that you have identified a **must-have** prospect. They're huge! They would help you **do** target in one hit so your bonus would haemorrhage like a magnum of champagne at a podium win. The volumes would **also** represent

103

significant growth to your company – making you look like a superstar. **And** the pull-through potential to attract other business is substantial. Are you with me so far? **This** is a wave prospect. In the surfing world you would have to go to Mavericks or Waimea Bay for something this big; once in a lifetime; must-have; **sexy!** What are you going to do – load the potential for success or failure with the Tier 1 on one generic roll of the dice? Go for 'dramatically reducing operating costs' and hope they take the bait? I know that failing here is not **the end**. You can approach others, and reapproach the CEO in a month because they won't remember the initial contact. But you want to take a rapid access approach. You want to shorten the sales cycle, not spend months trying to gain significant access.

So you make a few approaches further down the organization but without **selling**. Your approaches go something like this:

'Hi, how are you? Yes, I'm the guy from Crank Handle. Just thought I'd drop in. I've never spoken to you guys before. I brought some freebies along. Just wanted to get a feel for what you guys are doing. I've always been interested in meeting because you occupy such an interesting space in the market. What sort of stuff are you guys focusing on at the minute? We've got this big drive on efficiency and cost-base going on in our business. You know what directors are like...'

You can do this face-to-face, or by telephone (without the freebies obviously) or you can have some of your staff do the legwork. This might be field engineers, customer service staff or whoever. Get inquisitive – be **nosey!** Check with your colleagues to find out if any of them have contacts in the company. Of course, this works equally well in existing accounts where you want to gain access to the CEO. And perhaps along the way you *might* find that environmental responsibility and social conscience are marginally less prioritized than dramatically increasing turnover and in-line profit. Is it possible that some companies might publish statements to be perceived more positively by their customers so that they buy more? I have no idea. My interest is not in questioning the noble or ignoble intentions of man or womankind. I just think that in pursuit of our heart's desires it makes sense to back the right horse, or Benefit Pitch!

BENEFIT PITCH IMPACT

The Benefit Pitch should go off like a firework! And we're not talking about one of the skinny sausage-sized ones that go whizz–pop–bang either. We're talking about an ear drum splitter the size of your right leg. The first half of the Pitch is the **WHOOSH** as the rocket hurtles into the sky with eye-watering speed. This is the name drop or the piece of market intelligence. I want this part to create such a **WHOOSH** that they strain the muscles in their neck from involuntarily whipping their head round fast enough to follow the sound. This is not then followed by the 'pop' of the detonation. There is a moment; a pause; a fraction of silence; the calm before the storm and then:

B-A-N-G!!!!!

You go to firework displays. You know the kind of 'Bang' I mean. It doesn't matter if it's the worst-financed display in the history of things that go bang in the night sky; at least they spent some money on the last crowd pleaser of the evening. The sound reaches you just as the shock-wave knocks you off your feet. The cheap plastic tables and chairs are literally **blown away** and children scream in a moment of should-I-be-scared excitement. And as the sound dies, the impact is so shockingly powerful that immediately your brain disbelieves your senses in an *'It can't have been THAT BIG'* moment. But deep down inside you know it is. It's SO BIG that you can feel the aftershock in your liver!

Ladies and gentlemen: use the Benefit Pitch in a well-constructed and well-delivered way based on a highly topical point of interest and the impact should be significant enough that the Tier 1 prospect pauses for a moment... to identify the curious feeling in their liver.

DEALING WITH THE PA OR SECRETARY

These days it is uncommon to go straight through to a Tier 1 personality without first being screened. And the person who carries out this natural selection, the Personal Assistant or Secretary, is not someone to be taken lightly. A high percentage of their selection obviously includes screening **out** sales calls. Why? Because they've been told by the busy person whom they screen: '**NO** sales calls'. In Cascade Selling this particular Gate Guardian is as important as the prospect, because the Tier 1 Guardian has the *independent* power to deselect us.

This being the case we should treat them like the contact – they are that important. Unlike when dealing with a first-line Receptionist, you should Benefit Pitch the Tier 1 Guardian, with a modified version of the pitch that you will subsequently use with the Tier 1:

Tier 1 Guardian	'Good morning, this is Susan Young.'
Bona Fides	'Good morning. This is David Legg from REDSECTOR.
Modified Pitch	'Susan – we've been working with Crackerjack over the past six months to help them substantially reduce their operating costs and John Garey their MD suggested that we get in touch with Roger. Tell me, when will he be available to take my call?'

Deliver the pitch in an unhurried, calm and 'senior' tone. What will the Guardian do? Well anything *could* happen in the next half hour but at the very least you have created all the right conditions for the Guardian to play your pitch back to Tier 1 and give you a return call.

Further methods for enhancing our approach success-ratio are discussed in Chapter 8.

TRY IT – YOU MIGHT LIKE IT!

Whenever I train a group of sales people it's always a pleasure because sellers are normally a wide-awake try-anything-once bunch. It never fails to surprise me though how reticent some sales people can be when it comes to Initiating an Approach to new contacts, especially Tier 1s. Maybe it's the natural fear of rejection or failure in us all that raises its head every once in a while. But this fear or perhaps reticence will be noticeable on a call, especially to a Tier 1.

So before you decide to summon up the grit and bite the bullet, be advised: none of the techniques discussed in this chapter should be attempted until at the very least they **sound** good. It would be nice too if they could also be delivered with real confidence! So here are a few suggestions:

1. Show the techniques to colleagues in your team or next time you have a sales meeting do a one-hour session where everybody works up some pitches, and try them out on each other.
2. Each of you should work up five Tier 1 Benefit Pitches. Rehearse them. This means delivering them out loud until they **feel** and **sound** right. Remember to emulate the voice skills that are relevant to Tier 1.
3. Play the techniques back to each other and take a little constructive critique from your teammates. Their ears will be able to hear things that yours can't. Remember to brief them to receive your pitch as a Tier 1 Driver personality.

4. Create a central library of the good ones that everyone can use. Keep topping it up as you create new ones.

CHAPTER 5

STEP 5
HOW WILL YOU GET THEM TO REVEAL THE REALLY JUICY STUFF?

GAINING INITIAL COMMITMENT

Here's the bad news. Regrettably the pitch will very rarely motivate a prospect to throw back their arms and welcome the sales person into their business with a hug and a big wet sloppy kiss. Stop for a moment and look up: directly above any sales person during the Initial Approach is Madame Guillotine. The blade is sharp and shiny and quivering with each word that comes out of the sales person's mouth. The blade quivers ready to fall as a reflection of the often subconscious decision-making process going on in the mind of the prospect. As those seconds tick away they will debate: should I stay or should I go? Will I let this caller continue or shall I chop their worthless head off (emotive but true)? Am I **interested** or not?

I've exaggerated a little. Maybe one time in a thousand they'll give you a big wet sloppy kiss, if you catch the right person in the right place at the right time with the right pitch. What you *will* get from the pitch in 999 cases out of 1,000 is a prescribed response. It is this that we now have to deal with.

PITCH FLOWCHART

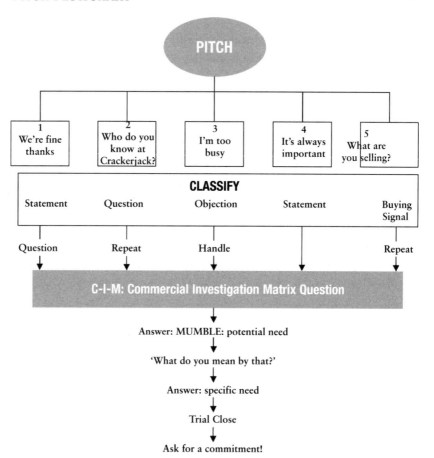

BENEFIT PITCH OUTCOMES

The purpose of the pitch is to get their attention. This is achieved through demonstrating that you've done your homework, that you have some current and relevant knowledge of their situation, and that you are talking their language. The potential outcomes of a well-delivered pitch can be fairly predictable. Take a look at the Pitch Flowchart on the previous page and examples 1–5. Each of these represents a common response – one of the range of comments that the pitch might produce:

1. We've just had a team of accountants in to rationalize our operating costs so we're fine thanks.

This is a *statement* as measured under the '**CLASSIFY**' line of the chart.

When the pitch generates this response ('No; that's not important') ask them: 'Well let me ask you this then: what **is** top of your list of priorities right now?'

And they might just tell you something that you can contribute to.

Then move onto the C-I-M.

2. Who do you know at Crackerjack?

This fazes many sales people. When they are making a pitch and get stopped, interrupted or **questioned**, many of them get a little lost and can be unsure of where to go next.

Tell them who you know at Crackerjack, then repeat the relevant part of the pitch.

Then move onto the C-I-M.

3. I'm too busy/ I don't take sales calls/ generally; Get Lost

This is an **objection**.

Handle it as per the system in Chapter 6.

Then move onto the C-I-M.

4. It's always important.

This is a **statement** with no rejection.

The real purpose of the Benefit Pitch is, like a Venus flytrap, to lure them in with the promise of honey.

If I was feeling daring I would be inclined to treat this as a **buying signal**. So move straight onto the C-I-M.

5. What are you selling?

Many sales people see this as a negative challenge or an objection.

I see this as the biggest **buying signal** on earth!

If you hear this from a Tier 1 Driver they are saying: **'Get to the point!'**

Repeat the relevant section: 'Well, we specialize in driving down business costs; so how important is overhead control to you right now?'

Then move on to the C-I-M!

WINNING THE APPOINTMENT

The first time that we use Cascade Selling with a prospect is likely to be while engaged in what many sales people feel is the most difficult activity: a cold contact by telephone. At this point we will be in pursuit of one of two things: either a face-to-face appointment or their permission to Cascade down through the business to do our fact-finding.

In order to get a Tier 1 Driver interested enough in making a commitment this early in the process we have to get them to reveal the beginnings of a problem that we can solve. As we've already discussed, this is a difficult job, for which we need a special tool.

HIGHLY SKILFUL QUESTIONING: THE C-I-M

The technique that I train sales people in to get prospects or customers to *willingly* (or perhaps maybe *unwittingly*) reveal problems is called the C-I-M: the Commercial Investigation Matrix. (Years ago I also heard a version of it called the Magic Wand.) The Matrix is a memorable and simple method of bringing out real problems within someone's job, department, company or market. Once problems have been uncovered, they need further questioning to establish their true extent and effects. This can be difficult, as initial questioning on sensitive subjects can be obvious or clumsy, creating resistance or mistrust. The Matrix is designed to ask the question 'So what are all your problems', but in a more skilful manner. The following example breaks the technique down into its component stages for illustration:

Stage	Technique	Wording
1	Preface	Tell me something Rebecca...
2	Trial closing question	If there was something that you could...
3	Variable	Improve/Change/Develop... (Select one variable)
4	Subject	About your XXXX... (Choose your **questioning subject**)*
5	Completion of trial closing question with an **open** question	What would it be? What would you choose? Where would you look? What would you consider?

* '**Questioning subject**' will be one of the usual areas in which your products and services can provide benefits. These might include, but not be limited to areas like:

– Business processes	– Productivity
– Production efficiency	– Budget management
– People effectiveness	– Expenditure
– Ability to win new business	– Disruption factor or costs
– Competitive edge	– Downtime
– Time management	– Performance

Some examples:

– 'Tell me something, Roger: if there was something that you could improve about your cost base, what would it be?'

– 'Tell me, Roger: if there was something that you could change about your competitive edge, what would you pick on?'

– 'Roger: if there was something that you could develop about the efficiency of your production operation, where would you focus?'

– 'Let me ask you this: if there was something that you could change about the general productivity of operations staff, what would spring to mind?'

This is a matrix question which means that it is many questions in one. If you multiply the number of variables illustrated in the model (three) by the number of questioning subjects (12), potentially you have 36 questions that you can ask!

The reality is that in any conversation the maximum amount of times that this technique can be used is three, and that's pushing it. As soon as the person that you're questioning picks up on the repetition they will think that they are being manipulated and then you might as well get your coat! Given the amount of drilling down that you can do into one answer (which we will discuss in this chapter), asking the question twice is probably a safe maximum; but I leave that to your discretion. However, just make sure that every time you ask the question you change the variable and questioning subject. Never use two the same in a row.

I would also advise against changing the wording of this technique 'to make it your own'. For example: 'If there was anything that you could improve...' or 'If there was one thing that you could change...' is not as powerful as 'If there was something...' If it's not broken, don't fix it.

EXPERIMENT – DON'T TRY THIS AT HOME!

Of course, the acid test for any technique is to try it out. It's important that it does not sound in any way contrived or scripted. It also has to be delivered in a conversational manner and at a conversational pace. This means that practice is required. The last place I recommend you do this is with major prospects or customers. They're too important to use as guinea pigs. So here's an alternative suggestion, and it will also demonstrate the awesome power of this technique to the non-believers: those of you who think it's too simple.

Cook your partner a candle-lit dinner. Get rid of the children (if relevant). Put on some soft music, and dim the lights. Wait until the starter and main course are finished and you're into dessert, because the best things happen over dessert after all. (If you're not married, be careful that you're not giving off entirely the wrong signals right from the start!) Wait until your partner does **not** have a mouth full of blancmange, gaze longingly into their eyes through the flickering candle flames and ask; 'Darling; if there was something that you could change about our relationship together, what would you pick on?'

Then duck! Told you it works...

AFTER THE C-I-M

If you ask a C-I-M and they reply that there is nothing that they would like to develop about the efficiency of their production operation, don't panic. Classically sales people can get a bit stuck here and without knowing it become a little argumentative: 'Are you sure? There must be something that you'd develop?' If the first C-I-M does not produce the required response, try another on a different subject: change the variable and the questioning subject and try again!

'Good for you. Let me ask you something else: if there was something that you could boost about the performance of the business, where would you start looking?'

You can change or remove the preface (see 'Attention Getting Techniques' below). Using it too frequently becomes an audible irritator. You can also use other variables. In my function I use 'Boost' just for an audible and non-repetitive change of scene.

The Matrix doesn't just have to be used as our leading question after the Benefit Pitch. It can be used at any point during the Needs Discovery stage before, during or after our standard questions. It is also highly effective as the first question of the face-to-face initial meeting with a prospect.

THE APPOINTMENT

Imagine that you have initiated an approach to David Jenkins the CEO of Roadrunner Distribution. Your business specializes in fleet maintenance and has a track record of streamlining fleet costs in large companies. One of your recent customers is Crackerjack Promotions, who you know is a supplier to Roadrunner. You get through to your target contact:

Answers	David Jenkins
Bona Fides	*Good morning. I'm Charlie Harper from Fleet Dynamics.*
Pitch	*David – we've been working with Crackerjack Promotions over the past six months to help them substantially reduce their operating costs. Tell me something: how important is overhead reduction in your business right now?*
Question	Who do you deal with at Crackerjack?
Answer	*I work closely with Phoebe Buffay the CEO.*
Repeat	*So tell me: how important is overhead reduction at the moment?*
Answer	It's always on our list of priorities.
C-I-M	*Well let me ask you this: if there was something that you could improve about the cost base, what would spring to mind?*

If you've asked a well-prepared question based on their 'Sand between the toes' (Business Wins) you might just cause their brain to start whirring instead of releasing Mme Guillotine on to the back of your neck! If you have caused a whirr – shout EUREKA! And as the echoes of your unadulterated euphoria die down, remember that if you've asked a thought-provoking question they'll need a moment to think so **shut up** and let them have it. Also you might hear some huffing and puffing. This is them debating whether they are going to tell you what they've thought of or not.

A typical answer might be: 'Oh, I don't know. I suppose it could be a bit tighter sometimes...'

This answer is classified as a **mumble**. It is non-specific and does not reveal a specific problem. The problem is only **implied** at this stage.

Sales people will often start closing at this point – unsuccessfully. You've got to build a little trust; you've got to get them to trust you enough to reveal the tip of the iceberg... the tip of a problem and 'it could be a bit tighter...' **is not it!**

I recommend when using this technique that every answer you hear you treat as a mumble, even if you think you know what their answer means. This removes so much dangerous assumption in selling and gives the Cascade sales person so much more information with which to work.

Your next question must be:

WHAT DO YOU MEAN BY THAT?

'What do you mean by that, David?' The subsequent answer is much more likely to reveal a more genuine need.

'I guess it would be nice if we could get the whole thing run a little more effectively.'

At this point in the Progression we move to the Trial Close.

However, especially when dealing with Tier 1s, prior to doing this the chances of success rise pro rata the more clearly expressed a problem is and, if possible at this stage, the closer we get to the cause. With the relative weakness of the last answer we might consider a requalification question: 'How do you mean?'

'Well,' David says after a pause, 'I think a lack of integrated supplier strategy probably isn't helping.'

TRIAL CLOSING AND GAINING COMMITMENT

We covered Trial Closing in some depth in Chapter 1. In this application the Trial Close is designed to **validate interest prior to** final closing or gaining the final commitment. We use 'If' or 'So if' in the following way:

'So if we could help you make that situation go away, would you be interested?'

'So if we could help with that, would you like to talk about it?'

'If we could show you a way to get rid of that issue, would it be worth your while having a chat about it?'

Remember once again that it is imperative that we get an emphatic 'Yes' before we proceed.

If the Trial Close produces ANYTHING OTHER than an emphatic 'Yes' answer

If a recipient of a Trial Close does not want to say 'Yes', they won't necessarily say 'No'. This is a confrontational word and many buying contacts will want to avoid getting into a fight, especially with a sales person! Sales people tend not to give up a fight easily. So a buying contact will say any number of other things instead. These include:

– Not really
– I'm not sure
– I'd have to think about it
– I might
– It's possible
– Maybe
– I'm not convinced
– Mmmmhhhh (non-committal throat sound)

I have observed many sales people over the years who automatically and very quickly come back with the equally confrontational 'Why not?' This immediately backs a buying contact into a pressure corner. To defuse this potential, our next step when we hear anything other than a 'Yes' is to ask in as calm and conversational a manner as possible one of the following:

– What else is important to you?
– What are the other things that you need to consider?
– What else do we need to talk about?

– What are some of the other priorities here?

– What else do we need to discuss?

The classic Golden Sales Rule then kicks in: **shut up and wait for the answer!** In a reasonably high percentage of cases it is likely that they will give you a more meaningful answer. Once they have done this you *might* summarize all the points raised in a Trial Close for a second time, gently.

But if they can think of one thing that is important to them then it's possible that they can think of two and maybe three. So the questioning needs to continue until all points have been uncovered:

What else is important?

And what else?

And what else?

Anything else?

Until we receive a 'No, nothing else.'

If you have uncovered all of their wants, needs and concerns then the law of selling averages says that you shouldn't receive negatives when you next Trial Close because there are no hidden objections to uncover.

When The Trial Close Produces a 'Yes' Answer

When the Trial Close produces a 'Yes' answer, our next step is to close for the commitment that we seek at this point in the Progression. In Cascade Selling with this scale of prospect the only commitment that we are seeking is either a face-to-face meeting or permission to cascade. This is not a close-for-the-order transactional sell.

It might also be possible to gain a commitment to a sit-down meeting there and then on a face-to-face cold call. A note to the sceptics here: I started life out as a pure cold calling sales person. I started in telesales, and then very quickly progressed into field sales. In a three-month period I face-to-face cold called every potential buying business in a three county area. I think wearing out shoe leather has always been a great way of identifying what potential business exists, unseen by the internet or business directory, in a geographical sales territory and it can bring you face-to-face with far more prospects than you would believe.

I am still a little surprised by the amount of sales people, including some of the 'senior' or 'experienced' ones, who reject and avoid cold calling. They claim a genuine dislike for the activity. In my experience cold calling develops and hones the skills and confidence necessary to go out there and **create** a major sales opportunity. It instils the cojones with which the most talented sales people appear to be gifted and with which they effortlessly topple the choicest prospect business. I agree that if you are targeting the Tier 1 of IBM, Sam Palmisano or Brendon Riley, or at Tesco, Sir Terry Leahy, *it would appear unlikely* that you are just going to walk straight into their office, put your feet up and have a chat. This logic then would suggest that there is no point in trying to telephone someone in that impregnable a fortress either. If you believe in this kind of assumption, you'd better call the €22 billion Tier 1 that Hans got through to and tell him to stop talking to sales people. However, there is also the fact that many sales people's Tier 1 contacts are far less elevated and daunting than a monster-big CEO, so the likelihood of being rejected on a face-to-face call is not 100 per cent guaranteed.

Every month I spend time coaching sales people to 'Kick down doors on trading estates' as one of my marketing colleagues loves to call it. A sales person and I go out for a day and take it in turns to initiate cold calls. Our objectives are agreed in advance: methods of dealing with barriers, Gate Guardians and objections are discussed and finally Benefit Pitches rehearsed. We rehearse these because we always get in front of a handful of key decision-relevant people! What a great way to sharpen the axe that we will need to get through Tier 1's door.

I don't know who invented the Trial Close but they did a hell of a job – it is incredibly useful in a wide range of sales applications (more to come). These days the Trial Close is in everyone's speech pattern. Every sales person has it in their vocabulary. All they have to do is use it deliberately at the right times.

WHY DO WE ASK QUESTIONS?

In the Cascade process the question that we ask next is critical! Sales people know how to ask questions but it's not the asking of questions that concerns me as much as the *answers*. Do the questions that we ask get the answers that we **need**? At a superficial level they do. We find out how many users will be involved and whether they will want product training, and what date the demo is booked for. I'm not talking about the surface level quantitative stuff. I want a lot more than that.

GET DIRTY

The questions that we ask are designed specifically to dig some dirt, right? If you're a Cascade sales person then you won't be presenting *anything* until you've dug up one or (preferably) more problems. Find something in their business that we can fix and we're a significant step closer to winning the sale, yes? In Cascade Selling, one of our biggest weapons is the question that gets them to reveal a problem. But prospects and customers aren't stupid. They know that you're quite happy to use the information they give you against them, so they play 'problems' close to their chest. Or, they live such pressured lives that they're not even consciously aware that they have 'problems'. They simply see a situation as normal: same-cr*p different-day.

THE PROBLEM

A 'problem' is defined as a situation that your product or service can improve. As discussed in Head Space (the Introduction) they typically fall under big headings like costs, sales, output, productivity, efficiency, performance and profit. The *problem* is that just finding something that you can improve does not make it a problem. In order for a prospect or customer to see an improvable situation in their business as a significant problem, they've got to **feel the pain!** The pain is the effect of a problem; its impact in their life, department or business.

This needs to be done subtly and skilfully and needs to drill deep into the cavity to be highly successful, especially at senior management level. Drilling down deep enough means that the pain you've got to get them to feel is the financial one. Every problem has **got** to be drilled down to a financial cost so that you can then present a powerful and believable financial argument (see Chapter 7). This **essential** 'drilling down' is in itself a highly skilled practice. But what we're concerned with first is initiating the questioning in a subtle and skilful enough manner so that we can get the prospect or customer to *willingly* reveal their problems.

THE SQIQIT SEQUENCE

The SQIQIT (Squeakit) Sequence illustrates the various stages of 'drilling down'. It is not essential that sales people carry the acronym around in their heads, but it is essential that they get used to gently conducting root canal work on a problem so that its owner recognizes the ultimate financial downside.

CATALYST	EXAMPLE/GIVES US
Situational question (C-I-M)	*If there was something that you could improve about production efficiency, what would it be?'*
	Gives us: potential problem
Qualification question	*'What do you mean by that?'*
	Gives us: cause/causes
Impact questions	*'What impact does that have on...?'*
	Gives us: ramification/ramifications
Quantitative questions	*'How many people are affected?'*
	'How much does that cost per hour?'
	'Which adds up to £20k? Is that right?'
	Gives us: genuine problem/problems
Interest questions	*'What would happen if that stopped?'*
	Gives us: recognized need
Trial Close	*'If we could help you make that go away, would you be interested?'*
	Gives us: buy-in

THE C-I-M: FIRST STAGE DRILLING

You approach the plant manager of a cement works.

Situational question/C-I-M: 'Tell me something, Penny. If there was something you could change about the efficiency of your maintenance operations, what would you look at?'

A typical answer might be: 'Oh, I don't know. I suppose they could be faster sometimes...'

The tip of an iceberg is revealed. We do not start selling products or services to speed up their maintenance operations – it's far too early! At this stage this is only a **potential problem**. The plant maintenance operations might be too slow but we need to find out. Your next question, to begin the drilling down process, might be:

Qualification question: 'What do you mean by that, Penny?'

The subsequent answer should reveal a larger section of ice: a genuine need. 'Well, it would be nice if the Maintenance and Repair Team got more of their workload completed on time…'

Requalification question: 'How do you mean?'

'In the past few months they haven't been finishing their repair assignments on time, so they've overrun on their maintenance schedules.'

THE INITIAL APPOINTMENT

In the event that you are Initiating the Approach, this is the likely point at which you would close for an appointment using the Trial Close. At very first contact Tier 1 personalities are not overburdened with long attention spans. Enough of the iceberg (problem) has been uncovered to suggest a meeting:

'Look: if we could help you with that Penny, would you be interested in talking about it? When would you like to get together?'

'What I'd like to suggest, Penny, is that we get together for 20 minutes and talk about how we might be able to help. How does that sound? When would be good for you?'

The purpose of the meeting is to drill down a problem to a cost and therefore a need. Once identified, we seek Tier 1's permission to cascade down through the organization.

As we have already discussed, there is an alternative to closing for an appointment with a Tier 1. We can seek their permission to cascade without the necessity of a face-to-face meeting:

> 'What I'd like is your permission to go away and talk to some of the relevant people, and then come back and present my findings to you. How does that sound? Who will I need to talk to?'

THE C-I-M: SECOND STAGE DRILLING

In-Depth Illustration: All the Way to a Cost

If you are going to go face-to-face with the Tier 1, at the start of the meeting you might wish to rekindle the embers of the telephone conversation:

'It's a pleasure meeting you, Penny. You will remember that during our last conversation you mentioned to me that in the past few months your maintenance people have been overrunning on their schedules. If I may I'd like to understand this point a little better.'

Us	**Impact question:** 'What **impact** does an overrun have on the business?'
Them	*'The plant can't get back on-line.'*
Us	'What happens then?'
Them	*'We incur cross-department charges and sometimes the company incurs customer penalties.'*
Us	**Quantitative questions:** 'How many times has this happened in the past quarter?'

Them	*'Only twice.'*
Us	'And what does a cross-department charge look like?'
Them	*'It's normally a charge of €1,000 per hour which is deducted from our budget.'*
Us	'And how many hours shutdown did you incur last quarter?'
Them	*'Well, it was eight hours per month.'*
Us	'So that's €24,000?'
Them	*'Yes.'*
Us	'And what penalties did you attract?'
Them	*'We had two in the past three months: Stonetek was €10,000 and Rockhound was €22,000. Rockhound was quite a large contract.'*
Us	'€32,000 in a three-month period?'
Them	*'Yes.'*
Us	'So what you're saying is that because your M&R team aren't finishing their workload on time, at the current rates, per annum it's costing €96,000 from budget and €128,000 in customer penalties. Is that right?'
Them	*'Yes. I guess it is.'*
Us	'What happens if you keep letting customers down?'
Them	*'Well obviously they complain... and some might try our competitors...'*
Us	'Has this happened recently?'
Them	*'Yes, we lost one last quarter.'*
Us	'What kind of spend level did they represent to the company?'
Them	*'They were worth about €250,000 a year to us.'*
Us	'So apart from the €224k in costs, you're also looking at an additional annualized €1 million in lost revenues, if one per quarter becomes typical. Is that right?'
Them	*'Yes.'*
Us	'What do you think is causing these issues with the M&R team, Penny?'

Them	*'Several of them have joined us quite recently and I'm not convinced that their skills are as well developed as we thought.'*
Us	**Interest question:** 'What would happen if the M&R team got back on track?'
Them	*'Well, there would be a definite financial benefit.'*
Us	**Trial Close:** 'If we could help you realize that gain, would you be interested?'

Remember: this is not the time to start final closing. One clearly identified need is good. But two needs are better, three better still. At this point we want to go and explore the rest of the operation to find the serious problems, needs and costs. We want permission to cascade to others. Additionally it goes without saying that at some point during the Initial Appointment (IA) they are going to want you to tell them who you are and what you do. I recommend keeping it brief and not talking in-depth about products and services. It is still possible for the sales person to get bounced out of Tier 1's office, never to be allowed to return, if the seller starts talking about operational factors outside the Tier 1's sphere of interest.

GAINING PERMISSION TO CASCADE

Gaining permission might sound something like this:

'What I'd like to do is go away and talk to some of the key people involved in this situation and see where we might potentially be able to help. Who would you suggest I talk to?'

Gather two or three names if possible, with their job titles.

'What I will also need is an appointment to come back to you and present my findings. Should I book that with you now or with your PA?'

Remember, ideally the appointment will be no more than about three weeks away, so that they don't forget who you are!

BEWARE OF GETTING DUMPED

Getting dumped is famous in the annals of traditional selling. I have observed transactional sales people brave or intuitive enough to attempt a Tier 1 approach. And some of the time they get through to the contact and pitch. At this point feel-good-factor rushes in, and while they're feeling all warm and fluffy about their achievement (making contact), the Tier 1 says: 'You don't want me: you need to talk to my production manager'. Something significant just happened; some sales people notice it and some don't. Whilst this might look and feel like cascading it is **not**, and deep down in the id they know it. You can officially call the motion Cascade when we request or suggest it. When they suggest it, it is called something else:

- Getting Dumped
- Talk to My Subordinate
- The Fob Off
- The Hand Off
- The Hand Me Down
- The Slippery Slope
- The Nose Dive
- The Crash and Burn
- Call the Fire Brigade
- The You're Screwed

Granted, I might have got a little carried away there at the end but you get the point. When you get fobbed off there is no path back. All they do is divert you off somewhere else, never to be seen again. And the fact that the Tier 1 told you to talk to someone else has no 'Open Sesame' effect when it comes to opening the door to them. Actually, often it's the complete opposite. There must be some Secret Squirrel Handshake or Joe 90 Password thing going on, because you never get to talk to the production manager. Maybe that person is an invented name specifically for cold callers. 'He' is the equivalent of the Recycle Bin. Mention that you're calling the production manager and everyone except you knows that he doesn't exist, but they still put you through to voicemail anyway.

If and when this happens, you have two choices. Either you can go with their suggestion (which is the point at which you exit Cascade Selling because your Tier 1 sponsor just got on the Big Yellow Bus), or you can treat the suggestion for what it is: a well-camouflaged objection: 'Thanks for the suggestion, David. Let me ask: who in the business has an interest in major profit gains?'

David replies: 'I do'.

You continue: 'When we find areas of major profit recovery, I'll need to report to you personally. I'd like to book a meeting for three weeks' time to do this, subject to cancellation if we find nothing. How does that sound? And who else do I need to speak with?' (Note the use of a '**Subject To**' Close).

Of course, there are no guarantees here, but you have to try, so be brave and challenge the objection. The reason that sales people get dumped is often because their Introduction or Benefit Pitch didn't get the job done. It didn't create attention and interest. Regaining your footing when the ground is falling out from under you is always difficult, and in real terms works so very rarely. Better to get it right first time with a highly targeted and polished pitch.

SALES QUESTIONING SKILLS

I have heard selling defined in many ways over the years; one of the most common definitions being either 'hard sell' or 'soft sell'. I'm sure that these phrases were originally coined based on something properly scientific, but I think that the real meaning has long since sailed down the plug hole. These days, when a sales person talks about the soft sell they typically mean a gentle approach designed to minimize conflict and objections. Hard sell reciprocally means going for the throat like a Rottweiler on a pogo stick.

Let's face facts just this once. There is no hard or soft sell. There is only skilful and unskilful selling. Skilful selling identifies the most expedient route between where we are now and where we want to end up. Unskilful selling bastardizes all the good stuff and dilutes the sales person's most powerful weapon: the humble question. In very simple terms there are two kinds of questions out there: you got it, Open and Closed. Sales people who use the 'soft sell' normally exclusively employ the Closed variety.

Open Questions begin with an interrogative and prompt an informational response. Closed Questions begin with an entirely different set of words and usually get a 'Yes' or 'No' answer. Take a look at the table on the following page.

Open Questions should produce an informational response. Open Questions begin with:	**Closed Questions** invite the other party to choose between alternatives: Yes or No. Closed Questions begin with:
– What	– Could
– Where	– Would
– When	– Should
– Why	– May
– How	– Do
– Who	– Will
– Whom	– Are
– Whose	– Is
– Which	– Can
– How many workstations do you need this month?	*– Can I ask how many workstations you'll need this month?*
– What sort of training will the operators need?	*– Will the operators need training?*
– How long before you'd like us to deliver?	*– May I ask when you'll want delivery?*

It's amazing how many sales people still default to the 'soft sell' and deliberately choose Closed Questions to try to minimize resistance. Or perhaps when they ask questions they have not deliberately selected Open Questions as the weapon of choice – the one that will deliver the better outcome.

Either way, Golden Sales Rule No. 749 in *The Selling Book of What's What* says: 'Sales people ask Open Questions because what they want is **information**. They avoid Closed Questions because they make it much easier for a buying contact to say "No".' The two exceptions to this rule are:

– We use a Closed Question when we specifically **want** a 'Yes'/ 'No' answer: e.g. the buying contact asks you if you can deliver next week.

You respond with the question: 'Do you want it delivered next week?' Often their reply can be: 'No. I was just asking.'

– **Or** we use a Closed Question when we are closing: 'Well, we've agreed the financials. On that basis then – is it a deal?' This is known as the Direct or Ask-For-It Close.

ANOTHER ACID TEST

Now, I know what you're going to say: 'I'm an experienced sales person – I know how to ask Open Questions!' And there are many who do, but humour me for a moment if you will. If, right now, you can rattle off ten Open Questions without even thinking about it then skip this next part and move onto 'Questions Complementary to the Interface Skills'. If you can't, what it says is that you probably don't ask them as often as you could.

Task: Write down the ten leading Open Questions that you want to ask when you are talking with prospects or customers. When you have refined the list either print it in pale grey or write it in pencil and put it inside your customer notebook or whatever you write notes in when you are selling. Use these when you are in your next sales call; your buying contact sitting opposite you won't be able to read them because, first, the only person who can read grey writing apart from you is The Man with the X-Ray Eyes. Second, **no-one** can read upside down without **staring at the copy really hard**.

QUESTIONS COMPLEMENTARY TO THE INTERFACE SKILLS

Now start thinking about the *Interface Style* of the person that you will be questioning. This will give you the opportunity to ask *Style Compatible* questions. Of the four styles two are logical (Driver and Analytical) and two are emotional (Amiable and Expressive).

It follows then that the most complementary wording for questions will play to the style of the individual: for the logical people we will use the word 'think' and for the emotional people 'feel'.

'What do you think about the sub-prime situation in the United States currently' is likely to get the Driver and the Analytical giving you their opinion.

'How do you feel about the humanitarian situation in Burma' is likely to get the Amiable and the Expressive expressing their point of view and emotions.

Just as with the Open Question list above you can also prepare thinking and feeling questions in advance.

ATTENTION-GETTING TECHNIQUES

It's a pleasure every once in a while to get back on the questioning track – asking the most productive questions in the right way! There's only one thing sales trainers don't tell you when they say to use a massively high percentage of Open Questions: the more of them that you use in a row, the more the conversation sounds like an interrogation. It's okay for the sales person but imagine what it's like for the poor buying contact. Once we have decided on the right type of question, we have to make sure that the way in which we ask it gives the other party the right feeling about us. In simple terms questions need to be easy on the ear and nicely conversational. This is done by *prefacing* questions with conversational phrases, cloaking or disguising the Open style of the question.

The most powerful preface is the imperative 'Tell me':

'Tell me, Jane: (PAUSE) **Who...?**'
'Tell me something, Roger: (PAUSE) **What...?**'

Beginning a question in a closed manner can also be used as a prefacing technique, because they will always answer the second question which will be Open:

'Could you tell me something Emma? (PAUSE) **Why...?**'
'Could we establish something here? (PAUSE) **When...?**'
'Would you mind telling me something? (PAUSE) **How...?**'

These examples utilize a double preface: a statement followed by 'Tell me':

'I'd be interested in knowing... (PAUSE) **Tell me: Where...?**'
'Now this is an interesting area... (PAUSE) **Tell me: What...?**'

Or without the 'Tell me':

'It would help me to know, Beatrice: (PAUSE) **When...?**'

The beautiful thing about the preface, especially in the imperative form ('Tell me') is that it *arouses* the attention of the listener: it actually causes them to stop and wait for the question! It doesn't get any better than that. If you want positive control and attention in a conversation, then this gets it for you.

EXPERIMENT – TRY IT OUT!

Try this on one of your colleagues at work. Wait until you're sitting around a meeting table and say to one of them: 'Sam, tell me something...' and then wait, and I bet you Sam will say 'Yes' or 'What?' or similar. This is Sam's expectation that she is about to be asked a question and now that you've got her attention **she wants the question!**

Critical factors

1. The technique has got to sound **conversational**. The 'Tell me' should be nice and informal with a genuinely inquisitive tone to it.
2. The **pause** is the critical part of this very simple yet powerful technique. It should be about one to two seconds in duration.
3. It's important not to **overuse** the technique. Anything used too often will quickly become an audible irritator. Use plain Open Questions interspersed with prefaced ones.
4. There are some countries where the expression 'Tell me' does not impact particularly well. It loses something in translation and sounds far too demanding, which, of course, should be avoided at all costs. It can be softened as illustrated in some of the other examples, but 'Could you tell me...' seems to be the most user-friendly.

HASSE HAS A GO

I was running a Key Account Management/Cascade Selling Skills training programme a while ago in Lausanne, for a mixed group of French, German and Swedish delegates. We had finished the KAM material and were immersed in the Cascade Selling stuff. During the Benefit Pitch session, one of the delegates, Hasse was fidgeting a lot. I thought maybe he needed another fix of nicotine from his Grov White (smoking substitute – like a miniature tea bag that you suck on but full of a tobacco product not tea leaves). When we moved straight on to the C-I-M he really started wriggling and I asked if he was okay, and he replied that he was. We finished the C-I-M and broke for lunch. He rushed straight out of the room. He returned about 20 minutes later, and with a big smile on his face came straight over to me.

'I thought that the last session was so good I just had to go and try it. I rang one of my big Tier 1 prospects that I haven't been able to convince to see me. I hit him really hard with a Benefit Pitch, and then drilled him down with a C-I-M!'

'And what happened next?' I asked.

'It was the C-I-M that really got him interested. I'm seeing him next week!' was the reply.

TRY THIS – YOU MIGHT LIKE IT TOO!

In Chapter 4 we suggested not using techniques until they **sound** good and can be delivered with confidence! So in the same way:

1. Work up a few examples of C-I-Ms that you can use. Rehearse them out loud. Try them on colleagues.
2. Keep rehearsing the sequence of Benefit Pitch through to C-I-M and then appointment getting until you are ready to go live – and then do it: don't delay or you will lose the impetus.
3. Getting a bunch of you on the phones making planned and targeted Initial Approaches is a great way to cement these skills. Do not expect that you will be an instant success on your first call, so keep trying, but Hasse's experience actually is not an unusual one. Try it – you might just like the results!

CHAPTER 6

STEP 6
WHAT HAPPENS WHEN THEY SAY 'GET LOST'?

There is no escaping this one: to be a talented pilot you have to be able to get the tyres on the tarmac without turning the aircraft into matchwood. To be a talented racing driver you have to be able to get past the chequered flag in front of everyone else. To be a talented sales person you have to be able to handle objections. It is a guaranteed fact that objections are going to happen; but why? Well, it doesn't matter how good you are in sales, there is no such thing as a 100 per cent rule: **nothing** works 100 per cent of the time. You can sell to some of the people all of the time, and all of the people some of the time, but you cannot sell to all of the people all of the time.

It is possible, however, to deal successfully with a lot more objections than you might think, but you can't do it blind. You can't just charge at the objection and hope to either scare it off or squash it flat. It's a bit like Starship Troopers: 'To fight the bug, we must understand the bug'. Before you can begin to handle an objection, first you have to understand it.

STOP THAT!

The first cause of objections is a lot closer to home than it should be. Ever wondered why objections tend not to happen in a sales environment until a sales person has said something? That's right; the receptionist was sitting there minding her own business or the prospect was doing something interesting and then: enter the sales person! After that, all hell breaks loose with objections buzzing around the place like flies.

Most things that happen in selling do so because of what a sales person does or does not do: or because of what they do or do not say. It stands to reason then that a percentage of the objections that we hear happen *because* of the sales person.

Classically, if I asked the question: 'What causes sales objections to happen?' the range of answers that I would get back would include: prospects receive too many uninventive or unskilful sales approaches; they think you are going to try to sell them something; they get bored fast; they don't like the sales person; you've caught them at a bad time, etc.

Would it be possible to avoid or prevent these objections if we changed our behaviour? Let's take a look at some typical examples from early in a traditional sales process:

Sales person actions	Behaviour that causes objection	Behaviour change to avoid objection
Tries to get into a prospect building via an intercom.	Fully introduces herself and her company, selling to the receptionist over the intercom.	Keep it very brief. Ask: 'Can I come in?'
Asks a receptionist for the decision-relevant contact's name.	Uses a long Closed Question.	Should use a short Open Question.
Makes pitch to a Tier 1 buying contact.	Uses a long product-based approach.	Make it short and get to the main benefit fast.
Pitch gets interrupted by the buying contact with: 'How did you get my name?'	Is intimidated a little by the interruption and says that it came from the receptionist, and then does not continue speaking.	Says that it came from the receptionist, and then either carries on with the pitch or moves into a C-I-M.

These examples are merely the tip of the iceberg. They illustrate the fact that there are a range of behaviours that sales people exhibit throughout the Progression, often unconsciously, that create defensive behaviour and spoken objections in others. What is the best way of identifying and avoiding these behaviours? As sales people we need to be more analytical about what we do.

Having others assess our activities (a sales manager, for example) is also very useful where they are qualified to do so. Again, talking with other sales people about what they do and how they do it has merit. But most importantly staying on a personally motivated development pathway of books, CDs, tapes, articles, courses, blogs and so on is the real answer.

And, you can adopt a sales methodology like Cascade Selling that has been designed specifically to minimize objections by refining our sales behaviour. Then we need to consider the Big Three:

THE BIG THREE CATEGORIES OF OBJECTIONS

This does what it says on the tin! After we have recognized the importance of our behaviour, brace yourself for another major revelation. Sales people hear so many objections that eventually they become desensitized to them. The objections start to sound believable. Of course the prospect is too busy; how silly of me. Of course we're too expensive; I should have thought of that sooner. Of course I should have put something in the post; they must be desperately short of reading material! As a result of this we start to accept the most common objections at face value: 'Call us back in six months'. And as a result we get locked into an endless cycle of call-backs that never amount to anything. Have you ever opened a prospect data record or picked up a record card that says you have called six times, and felt a certain deflation prior to calling them for the seventh attempt? Deep down inside you *know* that they are just going to string you along for *another* six months.

In the Approach Phase of the Sales Progression we use Benefit Pitches deliberately to defuse the initial objection. But here's a shocker: we're human and we don't always get it right! So let's categorize the objections that we hear to understand them better and give ourselves a greater fighting chance. There are three kinds:

REAL OBJECTIONS

Let's say that you call a prospect and are connected directly. You get halfway through your shiniest Benefit Pitch and they interrupt you: 'Greg, it's very nice of you to call. I've had the switchboard number diverted to my mobile phone. The company burned down last night so I don't think we're going to be needing anything thanks.' If they're standing there in the smouldering ruins of a once shiny building with their shoes covered in ash, it's quite possible that you just met a genuine objection.

Or: you telephone a prospect and they interrupt your Benefit Pitch saying: 'Greg, I'll stop you there if I may. I'm sat here with the Official Receiver so I don't think we're going to want to talk to you thanks.' My question is: is there such a thing as an *Unofficial* Receiver? If they are indeed sitting there with someone who has formal responsibility for winding up the business, it is entirely possible that this is also a genuine objection.

MISUNDERSTANDINGS

I would agree with you if you were to say that sales people are nothing if not professional wordsmiths. As a result there should never be any misunderstandings. We are the ones who are paid to communicate clearly enough to ensure that they don't happen. But be careful: there is a technique out there in which some buyers have been trained. It is known as Selling the Dummy or the Deliberate Misunderstanding. This is where the buying contact deliberately summarizes a deal incorrectly, often following a negotiation. You have agreed the final costing in percentage terms, while they insist on using numbers. Or you have used numbers, so they insist on using percentages. Either way, when the deal is confirmed in writing, they will come back to you aggressively with something like the following:

'Wait a minute. You say here that we agreed a unit price of £25,000! That's a lie: we agreed 25 per cent which is a unit price of £22,000. I've heard of sales people like you but I never thought I'd actually meet one – either you supply us for the agreed price of £22,000 or you can take your business elsewhere and I will write a letter of complaint to your CEO!'

It takes a **very** strong sales person to not eventually crumble and give in on the £3,000 difference per unit, especially if it is within their negotiating range. This is an intimidating technique. Of course, a senior manager might tell you to 'Just say no! We don't want to trade with that kind of customer thank you very much!' However, the sales person wants to win the business and learning how to play the game is crucial to long-term success.

So let's be a little more preventative. The sales counter-technique is to challenge their claim in a gentle and bemused you-must-be-mistaken manner, and then show/fax/scan and email them your notes (which you will have constantly shown them during the face-to-face conversation, having drawn circles and lines for emphasis). Then you stand your ground, whilst reassuring them gently but firmly.

EXCUSES

What percentage of the objections that you hear do you think are excuses? I reckon it's as much as 99 per cent! Think about it:

- Put some literature in the post
- We're very happy with our current supplier
- You're too expensive
- We had a bad experience with your company
- I'm too busy
- I'm in a meeting

If we have become desensitized to objections here's the thing we don't do any more: we don't challenge every objection that we hear as if it were the first time. What I really want to do is say: 'The hell with it: every objection is an excuse and what I want to do is catch them red-handed. Catch them in the lie… *but deal with it so skilfully that they do not lose face while the objection is overcome…*'

The way that we do this is not to meet every single objection head-on. I don't want to wrestle the thing to the ground and try to snap its neck. It's far too tiring and more often than not you get your own neck snapped. Much more effective than that is to **defer** the objection. This does not mean by ignoring it. I want to challenge the objection, expose it as an excuse (to me the sales person), be allowed to push the objection into the background where it no longer matters and then move the sales conversation forwards.

To do this we need a system that is simple, being easy to remember and use.

THE THREE-STAGE OBJECTION HANDLING SYSTEM

STAGE ONE: Always question the objection

It is very rare that any prospect or customer when objecting will give you the real reason for doing so: the cause. Often this is because they either think that such a revelation will weaken their position or get them into a fight. What they do is 'blow smoke' to obscure the real reason just as an army will lay smoke across the battlefield to hide the movement and true intent of troops.

Here's an interesting fact: it's impossible to put out (extinguish) smoke. If you want to get rid of smoke you have to find and put out the fire. Our job in Cascade Selling then is straightforward: find the cause of the objection! But do it in a non-threatening or non-confrontational way so that they feel comfortable with revealing it. Stage one is used to expose an objection that you think is not real, to buy additional thinking time (in pursuit of a resolution), and to get more information.

Whenever you hear an objection – question it. The phrases below are in everyone's speech pattern and are quite useful as a selection for most situations.

– How do you mean?	– Run that by me again...?
– Compared to what...?	– I'm not sure I understand...
– Compared to whom?	– What do you mean by that?
– By how much?	– In what way...?
– Could you be more specific?	– Do you want 60-day terms?

There are exceptions to every rule. The one objection I suggest you do not question is:

Objection: 'I'm too busy.'

Sales person: 'What do you mean by that?'

STAGE TWO: Register the objection and feedback significance

The next stage is then to write the objection down and give verbal feedback. Be **conversational**, not a sales robot. **Relax**: the calmer you seem, the more businesslike (and not sales-like) you will appear. This buys **you** thinking time and it communicates to them that you are listening. This builds credibility.

• I'll make a note of that.
• Let me write that down.
• I can see that this is an important issue.
• I understand your concern.
• Let me jot that down.

STAGE THREE: Answer it with one of three techniques

Technique 1 – The Statement of Fact: telling it like it is:

- *'Well, the reality is that whilst our product doesn't provide you with that particular feature, the way that we can actually offer you even greater benefit is like this…'*
- *'Well, I understand that the market perception is that only Krell Diagnostics offer double-buffer relay drive, but we do too.'*

Technique 2 – The Trial Close: the 'So If':

We have used the Trial Close on numerous occasions and here it is again. In my view this is the best, the shiniest, the most versatile closing technique in the world. It is useful for so many jobs. Here we use it for objection handling:

Objection: 'You're too expensive.'

'So if we can show you where we are really competitive, do you think we could do business?'

Objection: 'We had a bad experience with your company…'

'If we could show you how our service has changed in the past 12 months, would you consider looking at it?'

Technique 3 – The Rephrase: So what you're saying is…

The Rephrase is in everyone's speech pattern and is wonderfully versatile. You could defer plenty of objections using the first example alone.

Objection: 'We're very happy with our current supplier.'

'*So what you're saying is* that in order for you to consider doing business with us we'd have to offer you some fairly impressive reasons for doing so? *Is that right?*'

'*So what you're saying is* that to become your next supplier we'd have to show you a really attractive service advantage. *Is that correct?*'

The Rephrase always begins and ends with the underlined sections: 'So what you're saying is…', 'Is that right' or 'Is that correct?'

EXAMPLE OF THE THREE-STAGE SYSTEM

Action	Buyer	Seller
Objection/ Question	You're too expensive	Compared to what?
Information/ Another question	Compared to Krell Diagnostics	By how much?
Information/ Feedback	At least five per cent	Wow. Okay, let me make a note of that.
Technique 3	—	So what you're saying is that we need to be more competitive; is that right?
Answer/ Technique 2	Sure	Well look. If we could show you some of the areas where we actually save you more than that five per cent, would you be interested in taking a look?
Action	Okay	Demonstrate product or service differentiator

In the event that the buying contact agrees with your attempt to handle the objection – 'Yes, if you could show us major benefits I would be interested…' you have successfully deferred it, on the premise that when you come to present your proposition you will '*show them some major benefits*'. If you cannot, it is unlikely that you will win their business on anything other than price anyway.

If they say 'Look: Read my lips – I'm too busy!' then you might just have found yourself a real objection. If they are irritated I suggest withdrawal, and then to approach them again another day, of course.

The Three-Stage Objection Handling System illustrates a step-by-step approach to challenging and defusing a very high percentage of excuses in a sales arena. As quickly as you come to use this system you will realize that there are situations where you do not even require three stages. The opening moments of a cold call can be a tense time with objections potentially coming thick and fast. It is possible to move immediately to Stage three, and if one technique fails, to immediately try another. This technique is known as the:

SHOTGUN

A few years ago I was asked by a client based in north-west London to run a morning 'Telephone Appointment Getting' training session for the whole company. This was a small company designing and producing cutting-edge websites, with about seven staff including directors. The idea was that they would then all jump on the phones in the afternoon to get some sales appointments. They asked me if I wanted to stay and join in for the afternoon. I know what you're thinking: why would you want to do that? Been in the sun too long? With my early background in telesales I decided to stick around because team-cold-calling can be fun. In a short space of time I got through to the managing director of a division of Ricoh. Ricoh produce a number of products including cameras and photocopiers. I presented the MD with my very best Benefit Pitch: 'Jim (pseudonym), we've been working with our clients recently to help them dramatically improve their competitive position. Tell me something: how important is taking market share from your competitors right now?' Which I thought wasn't bad.

He replied, calmly and unemotionally: 'It's not.'

That shook me. 'Oh hell,' I thought. Forget the whole 'Three-Stage Objection Handling' thing! With a rejection this flat, hit the guy. **Bam!** Go straight to my favourite, the Trial Close.

(To this day, I recommend the Trial Close as the immediate-action response to a major early objection when prospecting. Challenge them: call their bluff!)

'Look: if we were in a position to help you really take the battle to the enemy, would you be interested?' I replied.

'No,' was his response. Cool as a refrigerated cucumber.

'Oh *hell*,' I thought. Next step... I'm desperate: Shotgun! Run two techniques back-to-back (or side-by-side).

'Okay. So what you're saying is that in order for you to even consider talking to us we're going to have to offer you some really impressive reasons for doing so? Is that right?'

'That'll get you, you bast**d,' I thought.

As calmly as if he were reading the Sunday newspapers and sipping a cup of Java he said: 'No; that's not what I'm saying.'

I had no choice. I carried on Trial Closing and Rephrasing, not because I was living the dream of 'Never Quit' but because he hadn't told me to get lost. The thing that was lacking in the conversation, apart from the remotest sign of interest of course, was any indication that he was getting bored, frustrated or angry. Typically **if you fail to overcome an objection on the second attempt you will hear get-off-the-phone anger welling up in their voice like bile.** But not this guy! I was amazed. Tier 1s **do not suffer fools or sales**

people gladly. Any MD would have disposed of me long ago – but this one hadn't and I was at a loss to do anything but continue to try handling his objections. And then the clouds parted and a ray of light illuminated me right before I was struck by lightning; a thought hit me.

My next question was: 'I don't suppose you've ever worked for Rank Xerox by any chance, have you?' I asked.

'How the hell did you know that?' he asked incredulously.

And then another thought struck me: 'And I don't suppose that you went through their sales training programme, did you?'

'What the *hell* have you got over there?' he interrogated me, 'The Who's Who of Ricoh Divisional Directors???'

Aaaaah! Then I understood. All I did was carry on: Trial Close – Rephrase – Trial Close – Rephrase. If you're a senior person in the copier industry the chances are that at some point you will have worked for the mighty Rank Xerox. And if you spent any time there it is quite likely that you went through the sales training programme. This thing is legendary. It is three months long; it's residential; and you can fail. It also produces some of the most disciplined copier sales people in the world! I have met former Xerox people some of whom loved it and some who hated it but the thing that they all seem to have in common (the ones that I've sold to anyway) is that you have to be **bloody good** to sell to them. They will put you through hoops of fire and keep saying 'No' just to grind you down. You have to **prove** to them that you've got the selling minerals to make it through, or they'll just reject you out of hand for being Mike Myers: **not worthy.** And this trial by ordeal takes some time.

In the end, the entire office of telephone callers in which I was seated had ground to a halt. They were all listening intently to the non-stop flow of Trial Closes and Rephrases. This went on for *45 minutes.* Eventually I had run out of ideas and fell back on a closing technique known as the Last Resort Close, so named because it only works when you use it as a last resort:

'Look Jim, I'm just about done here. Before I go...' This opening element is a technique known as the Columbo; named after Peter Falk's shabby detective who always trapped the villain as he was leaving the room for the last time with the immortal line 'one more thing'. 'Before I go, let me ask you this: what **DO** we have to do to get you interested in talking to us?'

At which point he said with a muffled chuckle, 'All right. Come and see me. Next Tuesday, 2 p.m.' All of this because at the very last minute, bloodied, bested and exhausted, I had thrown myself on his mercy (he thought). I told him that the people coming to see him would be our MD and sales director. He refused, saying that he would only see me. Of course, I told him that I was just in telesales and that nobody allowed me out. I didn't mention that I didn't actually work there and that what I knew about websites would fit conveniently onto the underside of a small espresso cup. Eventually he crumbled a little and said that he would see the MD and SD.

They told me some time afterwards that the meeting lasted seven minutes. It took seven minutes before he asked them to leave – only because they did not use the same selling style that I had adopted during the call.

There is an exception to every rule in the book. This one agrees with the saying: 'If at first you don't succeed, try, try again!' The mitigating factor in objection handling is the voice tone – when you hear anger or frustration it is time to change direction and do something else.

CLASSIC OBJECTIONS HANDLED USING STAGE THREE TECHNIQUES

The following are examples of objections that are frequently heard from decision-relevant contacts, especially during the delivery of the Benefit Pitch. Bear in mind that the benefit claimed in the relevant techniques is one that your products and services will need to be capable of providing, e.g. reducing operating costs. The examples do not include Stages one and two:

Objection 1: Put some literature in the post.

Counter: Trial Close – Look, if we can help you significantly drive down your operating costs, would you be interested?

Objection 2: We're very happy with our current supplier.

Counter: Trial Close – Look, if we could show you some really impressive benefits compared to them, would you take a look?

Rephrase – So what you're saying is that in order for you to consider doing business with us we'd have to offer you some fairly impressive reasons for doing so? Is that right?

Objection 3: You're too expensive.

Counter: Trial Close – If we could show you how cost-effective we really are, would you consider talking about it?

Rephrase – So what you're saying is that in order for you to consider doing business with us we'll have to show you some real added value? Is that right?

Objection 4: We had a bad experience with your company.

Counter: Trial Close – If we could show you what we've done to ensure that that situation can no longer happen, would you give us another chance?

Rephrase – So what you're saying is that in order for you to even consider doing business with us again we'd have to show you some really positive changes? Is that right?

Objection 5: I'm too busy (as mentioned in Chapter 5)/ I'm in a meeting.

Counter: Trial Close – Look, if we could help you significantly increase call-centre productivity, would you give us 20 minutes to talk about it?

If you challenge every objection that you hear, the real objections will be uncovered with no harm done. Misunderstandings will be clarified, and excuses will be flushed out like vermin in a forest fire, to be dealt with using the simplest of systems and techniques present in every sales person's skill set.

CHAPTER 7

STEP 7
HOW DO YOU GET THE BUYING ORGANIZATION TO BITE OFF YOUR HAND FOR THE PROPOSITION?

MIND YOUR LANGUAGE

This is a word of caution to all the sales people (and companies) who use the word *solution*. It has become a common word in the business dictionary, so much so that I defy you to sit in any meeting between a sales person and a buying contact and not hear it mentioned several times at least. It is so popular that companies use it in their front line marketing messages:

Waste management solution
The solution to your needs
Our solution includes…
We offer a range of solutions to the oil and gas industry
Solutions for Operators and Manufacturers
Learning and development solutions…
A World of Engineering Solutions
Your Partner in Software Solutions

From literature to websites to the spoken word, solution is endemic. During the course of every working day, sales people skirt around the mines in the selling minefield. There are issues that are explosive and that can kill the sale. The Decision Making Unit is one of those issues. Ask about the DMU in the wrong way and your contact will shut you out. But sales people also create their own mines. There are things that sales people say that are explosive. Trigger Phrases during the Initial Approach are explosive. They can kill attention and interest. Solution is explosive too. Buying contacts cringe when they hear the word, for three reasons. First, the word is jargon which is unpopular at the best of times. Second, it's been so chronically overused that it has become meaningless. And third, **there is *no such thing as a solution* until you have first found a problem**. In the mind of the buying contact they either don't know or don't believe that they have a problem. Our job as Cascade sales people is to help them see the problems. So if we start talking about a solution before any problems have been uncovered, how will the buying contact react?

First they will feel B-O-R-E-D. Then a red flashing light and irritating buzzer will go off in their head every time the word is said. B-O-R-I-N-G!

Then they will formally get irritated and shortly thereafter terminate the conversation, meeting or picnic (depending upon the stage that has been reached in the Progression. Picnic is obviously a highly advanced stage).

You will note that getting the buying organization to bite your hand off for the proposition is referred to in the Sales Progression as 'Present Proposition'. It is not called 'Present Solution'. This specific language is used to ensure that the sales person adopts a vocabulary that is as non-irritating as possible right from the outset of the process. Talking about solutions should only begin once the sales person has established the buying contact's needs through helping them see their problems and the cost of those problems.

GENERIC OR CORPORATE PAYBACK MODELS

Over the years I have seen many versions of the Payback Model. You will also have heard them called *Financial Justifications*. They are always very sexy to look at, have the selling organization's logo all over them, have multicoloured boxes at every turn and present what is believed by the sellers to be a *must-have* proposition.

But buying organizations switch **off** the moment they see a Financial Justification. The reason is that they see it as nothing more than a selling tool because, first, it is too showbiz (glittery and shiny) and secondly it is not based on specific financial information from within their own business; it is based on generalizations, industrial norms and the selling organization's general experience. This generic model lacks credibility so buying organizations automatically think that the numbers suck!

THE REAL MUST-HAVE PROPOSITION

Imagine that you have gained access to a prospect organization at Tier 1 level, and that the CEO has given you permission to cascade down through the business. You have spent three weeks meeting with a variety of decision-relevant contacts, broadening your knowledge of the DMU at every step. In conversation with each of them you have asked a number of Commercial Investigation Matrix questions, and drilled the answers down to problems and the cost of the problems. Obviously you focus on the problems that you can solve through the provision of your products and services.

You've got to record the information as you go along (if only as an aide memoire) so you choose a straightforward spreadsheet package and you list all of the relevant information. It might look something like this:

	A	B	C	D	E	F	G	H
1	Cost-Benefit and Payback Analysis							
2		Units	# People	Hrs/day	Days pa	Hours pa	Unit cost £	Total
3								
4	INTERNALLY IDENTIFIED GAINS/ BENEFITS							
5	Design error reduction		3	2	232	1,392	18	25,056
6	Reduce visualisation skills		3	1.5	232	1,044	18	18,792
7	Remove manual bill of materials		1	3	232	696	18	12,528
8	Pre-tooling prototypes	10					1,500	15,000
9	Parametric BOA changes		3	1.5	232	1,044	18	18,792
10	Internal & external communications		4	0.5	232	464	18	8,352
11	Changing product sizing		3	2.25	232	1,566	18	28,188
12	Reduce the risk of problem products		1	0.75	232	174	18	3,132
13	Scrap bill re: design	1					14,000	14,000
14	Outsourced design staff/ project staff						9,135	9,135
15	Design overrun-induced TTM deadline shortfall						200,000	200,000
16	Remove need to inc overhead by extra designers		2				34,560	69,120
17								
18	* Estimated 7 working hours per day							
19	* Designer estimated @ £18/ hour overhead							
20	TOTALS						6,380	£422,095
21								
22	ADDITIONAL BENEFIT/ GAIN							
23	Speed up design process	20%						
24	Removes need for 3 design views	33%						
25	Time to market	10%						
26	Archive design faults	10%						
27								
28	ANALYSIS							
29	Cost of PROPOSED solution: £	15,000						
30	Cost of current practice p.a.: £	422,095						
31								
32	PAYBACK PERIOD (MONTHS)	0.43						
33	PAYBACK PERIOD (DAYS)	0						

This is a real spreadsheet used in exactly the manner described above, and comes complete with a mathematical error (I'm told). If you are a Sudoku fan, knock yourself out trying to find it. This one comes from some Interim

Management work that I did with a sales team in the Computer Aided Design industry in the UK a while ago. We were selling to a company in the aerospace sector, and met with a number of departmental managers. We discussed with them the downsides of their existing 2D CAD system and the upsides (in their view) of a replacement 3D CAD system. CAD software is used by designers in the creation of new products and the benefits of a three dimensional design environment over a two dimensional one are huge. Some of the language here is a little CAD industry specific, but take a look.

COST-BENEFIT AND PAYBACK ANALYSIS

Cost-Benefit Analysis is a formal tool used to assess the case for a business proposal by a buying organization and involves comparing the costs against the benefits. In my experience it is rare, however, that a buying organization will produce as in-depth an analysis as a selling organization. Face it; it's in our interest to be thorough – the greater the cost of the problems the faster payback is achieved. As a Cascade sales person you also need to be bold and investigate as many areas as possible. I have seen simple CBAs identify problems valued at millions!

'Internally Identified Gains/Benefits' in the left hand column lists all of the 'problems' found: all of the issues with the 2D product that the 3D proposition can fix or improve upon.

In order to accurately identify costs we measure: units, the number of people involved, number of hours per day, days per year, hours per year, separate unit costs and total costs. In the top header bar at line two these factors are represented.

So for example: one of the internally identified gains was Design Error Reduction. It was identified that three designers were wasting two hours a day each for 232 working days per year on design errors. This equated to 1,392 wasted design hours per year. At a unit cost of £18 (this figure was specified by the manager being interviewed) the saving, if the issue was corrected, would be £25,056.

The rest of the columns carry a range of figures representing other costs over time. In the case of CBA we show costs measured over the longest believable period which is a year. This corresponds with a company's standard financial planning period (cost per annum) and for our purposes magnifies the cost to its largest credible size.

'Additional Benefit/Gain' lists other areas of benefit achievable but in this case without the numbers to back them up. This is because the departmental manager being interviewed didn't want to release them. It transpired much later on in the sale that the reason for this was because he was the person who had sponsored the purchase of the 2D system only 18 months earlier, even though the 3D system was also available. No-one on the selling team decided to push for the numbers as they had no desire to make the manager righteously indignant.

'Analysis' outlines current cost versus the solution cost (for removing the problems).

'Payback' is the simple maths that identifies how quickly their purchase cost is paid back after the acquisition is made. You will note that the Payback Period in this example is nine days. Nine days after the new product goes on-line it didn't cost them anything!

'Subsequent Profit Recovery' says that in the balance of Year One, after the first nine days, the company recovers the Cost of Current Practice minus the Cost of Proposed Solution, which in this example is just over £407k.

While we are focusing on the financial impact in this example let's not ignore the fact that along the way 6,380 hours are also part of the saving! If you could help a company recover this many hours it might be fair to claim that the productivity gain and operating cost reduction properties of your 'Solution' are of epic proportions! A strapline that I would be tempted to use in subsequent promotional literature and Cascade Selling messages would be:

We've been working with PocketRocket Aerospace to help them create thousands of additional working hours. Tell me: how important is productivity gain in your business right now?

PAYBACK PERIOD

I have heard many sales people refer to this tool as a Payback Forecast or Return on Investment (ROI). Technically speaking ROI is measured by percentage but I think the term is generic enough for it to be used in this application without any fatal misunderstanding on the part of the buying organization. Many Tier 1s that I have worked with have willingly accepted the document shown as an ROI.

28	ANALYSIS		
29	Cost of **PROPOSED** solution: £	15,000	
30	Cost of current practice p.a.: £	422,095	
31			
32	**PAYBACK PERIOD (MONTHS)**	0.43	
33	**PAYBACK PERIOD (DAYS)**	9	
34			
35	**SUBSEQUENT PROFIT RECOVERY**		
36	Profit recovered after Payback period: rest of year 1	**407,095**	

As impressive as all of the numbers are, none is more so in my view than the Payback Period. The example shown is a conservative spread sheet compared to some with which I've worked, but the payback is a real sales asset. Only nine days, and the cost of the solution cancels out!

After that, the financial difference can be counted as profit recovery. This can be related at middle management level as equating to the cost of a beneficial purchase for the department, e.g. additional employees (salary), tools, process equipment, computers, etc. Additionally, when relating the cost (or in negotiating, the cost difference) of our solution it should be measured over the smallest period of time, e.g. per day over a financial year, or indeed over the life of the product, say, three years.

In this case the cost of the solution (rounded down) is £64 per working day (232) or £41 per day (365). Over the three-year life of the product it would be £21 and £13.

'The cost of recovering £407k in profit is £13 per day...'

GENERIC CALCULATION EXAMPLE

You have identified that you are replacing light bulbs with a greater degree of frequency than you would like. In the past two months you have replaced the bulb in the table lamp in the lounge twice:

Issue	Area	Unit Cost	Qty/month	Cost/year £
Light bulb	Lounge	£ 0.60	1	7.20

So, you spend £7.20 per year on light bulbs for the one table lamp in the lounge. However, you have six additional table lamps in the house, all of which need replacing with the same frequency:

Issue	Area	Unit Cost	Qty/month	Cost/year £
Long life bulb	House	£5.00	7	35.00

So your expenditure on bulbs is £50.40 per annum. What would the financial impact be if you replaced the bulbs that you use with a long life product that is guaranteed for one year?

Then the Payback Forecast looks like this:

Issue	Outcome
Cost of existing method	50.40
Cost of new method	35.00
Payback Period	8.3 months (35/50.40 x 12)
Cost saved £	15.40
Percentage saving	30.6

Granted, who can be bothered to think about light bulbs in a deeply serious way? And £15.40 saved over a year isn't really that much is it? But translate this through to a commercial environment. Talk to any company about saving 30 per cent on an operating cost and they'll be all ears. Even using the light bulb example, imagine an office environment where desk lamps are prevalent. The example could look like this:

COMMERCIAL VERSION: THE TWILIGHT ZONE

Picture a design office with 200 workers, each of whom has a desk lamp using a normal bulb, replaced with the same frequency as the household variety. You have entered the Twilight Zone. If we're picky the reality is that they probably replace bulbs more often due to the high level of use. For this example we'll keep it constant with the household, but any change would show through dramatically (in our favour) in the end figures.

Issue	Unit Cost	No. of lamps	Qty/year	Cost/year £
Normal bulb	£0.40	200	12	960.00
Replace bulb (wasted labour)	£0.53 (5 mins @ salary cost of £12,000 per annum)	200	12	1272.00
Reduced productivity	£189,000 200 hours 200 people made the company £5m gross profit last year. 378,000 man hours x 200 is 0.05 per cent productivity waste			189,000.00
TOTAL				191,232.00

Five minutes have been allowed to replace a bulb, which might be generous. You go from your desk to the store cupboard say, talking to a co-worker along the way. Perhaps you make a cup of coffee. Over a year, bulb failure and the time and productivity associated with it costs the company £191k!

Issue	Unit Cost	No. of lamps	Qty/month	Cost/year £
Long life bulb	£3.50	200	1	700.00
Time to replace	£0.21 (2 mins)	200	1	42.00
Productivity	6.67 hours			6,303.15
TOTAL				7,045.15

Replacement cost is like-for-like but only two minutes are budgeted for replacement as it is 'supervised' or a spare bulb is held at each desk.

Issue	Outcome
Cost of existing method	£191,232.00
Cost of new method	£7,045.15
Payback Period	0.4 months (8 days)
Cost saved/ subsequent profit recovery	£184,186.85
Percentage saving	2714.3

In this example we have identified some of the potentially substantial hidden costs behind what is a simple daily issue in any office: changing a light bulb. Even if you don't believe the productivity argument, there are those that will, especially if they are interested in productivity enhancements. Discount the productivity figures and the payback is still impressive. These types of arguments appeal specifically at Tier 1 and board level where any acquisition should be backed up by a Payback Forecast.

HOW TO USE THE PAYBACK SPREADSHEET EFFECTIVELY

There are several ways of creating a *must-have* proposition.

Prospect Tier 1:

At the end of the three-week Needs Discovery period you go back to the Tier 1 and attend the appointment that you made prior to cascading. Remember that you asked for Tier 1's permission to go away and talk to a few people to see if you could bring about the same substantial level of reduction in their operating costs as you achieved with Crackerjack. Of course, you didn't just talk to the people that Tier 1 suggested, you also talked to as many other decision-relevant contacts as you could uncover.

During the course of these interviews and as a part of your research into the business you discovered that the CEO set a growth objective for the year of £4 million with in-line gross profit at 10 per cent.

You sit down with Tier 1 and present your CBA/ payback spreadsheet:

'Well, Roger; it's been an interesting three weeks. We have interviewed the directors, departmental managers and staff on this list (give him a list) and have identified that in nine days we estimate that we can help you stem £422k in costs. In just over 11 months we can then help you recover £407k in lost profit, which I believe equates to your sales growth profit target for this year.'

Or you sit down with a prospect middle manager:

You fail to gain access to Tier 1 on your prospect approach and have to gain entry lower down the line of decision-relevant people. You are dealing (against your better judgement but you felt that you had no choice) with a middle manager. You gain access to the people that she authorizes and discover needs. You present the information that you have uncovered back to her in spreadsheet form:

'So Gretchen: these are some of the areas where our products can add benefit to your business and they add up to a £400k gain. I know that you said to leave this with you so I'll come back to you in a few weeks time.'

What will the middle manager do with that spreadsheet? Every manager in the world will be tempted to do this – Gretchen goes along to see the Tier 1:

'Boss: I've been doing some digging to see if we can really tighten the operation up to produce some savings and I've come up with this. I reckon that if we upgrade our design software (or whatever) it will pay for itself in nine days and in the balance of the first year after that we will recover £400k in lost profit. This is also the equivalent amount of profit that we would get from the sales growth targets that you set.'

I'd love to tell you that it's that simple! Tier 1 happily says 'Oh Gretchen, you're my hero!' But Tier 1 smells a rat. He knows that Gretchen doesn't use this kind of financial analysis tool and wonders where the hell the information came from, so he asks about it. But because you ran Gretchen through the spreadsheet she knows who or what the problem refers to, and which internal contact raised it. Tier 1 has no choice but to believe that the middle manager has just produced a qualified payback spreadsheet.

Or you sit down with a customer middle manager:

You are locked into middle management in an existing customer operation, and they won't let you gain access to more senior people. Give them the spreadsheet and see if they don't do exactly what the prospect middle manager above does.

PRESENT PROPOSITION

I have asked a number of hard-nosed Darth Vader-type CEOs what they would do if they were presented with such a qualified payback spreadsheet from a member of their own team. Every single one of them replied: 'I'd bite their hand off for the solution!'

Even if that is their immediate reaction, of course they won't. This is where the hard work really begins. Now you have to show them that you have the ideal product and service solution. You have to go back to all the people that you interviewed and show them how you can solve their problems. You might do this on an individual basis, by group presentation, benchmark, demonstration or trial. They in turn will feed back to the Tier 1 and he or she will put a tick in the box next to the problems to be solved in their area until the entire payback spreadsheet has been validated.

Our proposition or indeed solution is in three parts. The first part is the proposition that we make during the Benefit Pitch. We suggest to them that we might be able to deliver a sizeable benefit for them because we have done it, say, for someone else that they have heard of. The second part of the proposition is the Cost-Benefit/Payback Analysis. Everything in the Progression is designed to get us to the moment when the Tier 1 sees the scale of what we might be able to provide both them and their organization. This is the ultimate 'sand between the toes'; the true Buying Win. In doing so we dangle the biggest carrot imaginable: financial, operational and people improvement. The more the merrier! Tier 1 isn't interested in your products or services – they employ others to be expert in those areas. The third part of the proposition is when you present the relevant products and services to those people to validate the payback claimed. If you then also relate the payback to their strategic objectives (business growth, growth in new markets, shareholder value or whatever it is that they seek) then you might just get the great big wet sloppy kiss that you have secretly been yearning for since Chapter 5.

Approach a major sale (or any other kind) using Cascade Selling and you provide the most powerful sales sponsor, Tier 1, with both business and personal wins through Payback and Interface Skills. In doing so you just left the world of the sales person and entered the world of talented business person. In the eyes of the Tier 1 you become valuable. You become not an external supplier but an essential internal asset in the smooth operation of their business. You are seen as the most cost-effective efficiency consultant in the world; a trusted partner. Do the same with the other levels of decision relevance, adding product and service demonstration ('At last' I hear you say), and you build the same long-term value bridges with them too.

Every once in a while in the selling profession you catch a glimpse of all too illusive perfection and this is probably as close as you get to it. Like most sales people and especially as a sales manager and trainer I'm never satisfied: I always want better and more. So how on earth do you improve on perfection?

Turn the page.

CHAPTER 8

THE POWERHOUSE SUPPORT TEAM!

TAKE THE BEST THAT MARKETING HAS TO OFFER AND COAT THE TIP OF YOUR ARROW WITH IT – THE PROMOTIONAL APPROACH

Once we've got a high value prospect in the cross hairs, I think that there is a lot more that we can do to get their attention and interest. Yes, we can leave it all to the sales person, but with new business of this scale I want to reduce chance and increase certainty as much as possible. The hell with it: I want some **magic!** If only there was a bit of Voodoo that would help us here: some subliminal jiggery-pokery to make it easier to get to the Tier 1 contact, to get us fewer early objections, to even make the CEO **want** to talk to us (now I'm being silly), **or even...** (crass stupidity alert) **pick up the phone and call us**.

FORCE MULTIPLICATION

For my money, telephone and face-to-face approaches when made cold are still worth their weight in gold. And I love the whole 'Ramp It Up!' philosophy, latterly called the Force Multiplier. I love it even more when the cost of achieving the 'ramping' is relatively similar to the price of a bag of chips. Sales people benefit from taking a leaf from the marketing book and turning one of *their* key assets into a Cascade Selling strength. Let's look at tactical marketing. Classically this is the practical stuff that marketers do: designing and running advertising, creating brochures, sending out mailers, lead generation, etc.

The element of tactical marketing that I want to focus on is classically perceived to be low in the marketing food chain: promotional items or goods. These are things like pens, highlighters, clocks, baseball caps, umbrellas, mobile phone hammocks and so on. We all get to see a lot of this stuff – in many organizations they pump it out as a cheap method of reaching out and touching prospects and customers and communicating a **tiny** message (how much message can you get on a pen?) or '*The Brand*'. Walk into any High Street bank and you can pick up cheap free pens by the bushel!

This is where I think these organizations and marketing as a general function undersell.

If you've got a marketing department, or even a marketing person, then you've already got a resource and expertise head start. But in truth you don't need either. When it comes to tactical marketing in the pursuit of new business, I think some of the most talented protagonists are sales people when they discover which end is 'up'. In fact, while this subject is officially the domain of marketing they tend to follow more of a general marketing direction which is out of whack with closely targeted sales and prospecting.

PUMP UP THE VOLUME

Put simply, what I want to do is take death-by-ten-billion-ballpoints and turn the volume **right** up! Think about what your company sends out, and let's broaden the mix by adding all the other stuff that you use to reach out and touch prospects and customers. You know the kind of thing: email, letters, newsletters, brochures, etc. Now you might say that your company already sends this kind of stuff out by the container-load and the results are somewhere between middling to fair to a complete waste of time. And that's as it should be, because typically when you mail out anything like the material above don't be surprised when you get an average success or response rate somewhere between 0.1 per cent and 1 per cent.

ONCE YOU POP YOU JUST CAN'T STOP

But we're looking for magic, so forget the whole idea of mass mail-outs, in whatever form. If we're going to utilize this promotional material to maximum effect there is a shortlist of critical factors that have to be observed:

1. Promotional items must be sent to named contacts.
2. Make sure you know their job title.
3. Where possible, mailed items should be marked 'Private and Confidential'.
4. Items should be mailed against a database (see 'Campaigning').
5. Never send a feature-oriented brochure. Brochures are boring, especially for Tier 1.
6. Never send a long rambling formal letter (but you can send a Benefit Pitch letter).
7. Forget brand awareness: avoid sending items (a pen, for example) that just has the business brand and phone number/web address on it.
8. The message that you communicate must be the right message for the right contact or level of contact.
9. The message must be short and punch in a contact-relevant benefit.
10. Think 'Pringles': once you pop you just can't stop. Keep drip-feeding the campaign.
11. So identify a range of promotional items to send out one at a time, over a given time period or frequency.
12. Inexpensive is good; cheap or tacky is not. Inexpensive, creative but useful is superb.
13. Innovative is fantastic. We want to get their attention.
14. They are unlikely to respond to the first item so you have to drip feed them with different items and a variety of relevant messages.

15. So that when you place a call to them they recognize your name and let you through! (Don't pull faces; this happens.)

16. Or (dare I say it?) they 'admire' your persistence (this also can happen).

17. Or, when they actually decide that they are in-market and want to talk to potential new suppliers they have to call you first because yours is the name that's been fire-branded into their consciousness.

I want your Cascade Communications to scream. If cheap pens are a whimper then I want a bang from your Cascade materials.

MESSAGE IN A BOTTLE

The first thing that you want to decide is which promotional items you are going to invest in. The simple way of doing this is to brainstorm with your team 12 promotional items (that's one a month for a year) that are as innovative as possible. Or call in a promotional goods company to present their low-cost but high-impact wares at your next sales meeting. The best one I have seen recently is a milk bottle sent by post in a cardboard box with a piece of paper rolled up inside it. When I was shown the box I HAD to open it. When I saw the bottle I was bemused. When I saw the piece of paper rolled inside the bottle I **had** to take it out of the bottle and **I had to read the message**. I couldn't stop myself; I was compelled. Well done to Gary H. and team. That's innovative.

'Useful' would be something that the recipient could use every day: a particularly stylish mug (there is a heat sensitive mug on the market which is blank until it is filled with hot liquid whereupon it reveals its message), a mouse mat, a ruler, rubber duck, etc. Be advised that this stuff can get expensive if you're not highly selective.

However, 'Tasty' seems to get good results too: a sachet of particularly fine

Triple Chocco Mindblower Hot Chocolate or Double Espresso Java Headbanger Coffee. Perhaps even a stylish snack-size chocolate bar produced by one of the finer chocolatiers? These would need to be accompanied by your message on a compliment slip (or perhaps a photograph or even a 3D rendering of the message), but who can resist chocolate?

A great one that we came up with in Hong Kong was a large photograph. I was working with a client team who wanted to break into a number of major retailers. We walked through a large multistorey shopping mall and from the central atrium area saw the retail premises of Starbucks Coffee. On the next floor directly above it sat a Pacific Coffee store. The company wanted to introduce their product to Pacific believing that it would help them increase consumer-throughput. At the time Starbucks had by far the dominant market share. So the idea that we came up with was to send the CEO of Pacific a large (30cm x 30cm) framed photograph of one outlet above the other, with a choice of slogan:

Want to rise above Starbucks in the battle for market share? Call Alan on...

Or:

We specialize in helping HK companies dramatically increase their attraction of new consumers. How interested are you in growing market share **fast?** To discuss, call Alan on...

THE MESSAGE

This is where the success or failure of the approach and indeed the entire campaign is forged. The statistics on mail-shotting anything that involves the written word are quite explicit: you've got an *average* of one second and a maximum (if you follow Benefit Pitching) of *maybe* three to four seconds to hook the recipient or reader; to get their attention and interest. You know what it's like – you receive an innocuous or non-source-specific letter; you open it and unfold the contents. Inside one second you have seen the word 'Loans' and as you are not in the market for a loan the screwed-up ball of paper is rolling around the rim of the waste paper basket in the greatest slam dunk point that you scored since the last piece of junk mail you opened. One second!

Using this methodology with your promotional material becomes even more refined. When you send out any promotional item you have a choice of messages: either you can send out a Benefit Pitch – or you can send a Benefit Question. The Benefit Pitch is reasonably long when written and can go either on the item or accompany it. The Benefit Question is much shorter and often intended for smaller promotional items – mainly because you'd need a pen the size of a baseball bat to fit a Benefit Pitch on.

Also the messages that you use are likely to focus more on Generic appeal because Name Dropper and Market Intelligence Pitches are often better conducted on a case-by-case basis. Remember: the message has nothing whatsoever to do with products, services, features or brand! It has got to be a key Buying Win that you can deliver and that is **totally** relevant to the tier or title of the person whom you are mailing. Also, whatever you claim, you have to be able to substantiate it from what you have achieved with other customers.

Here are some examples of Benefit Questions:
- Want to reduce your business costs by 12 per cent?
- Want to slash operational downtime by 14 per cent?
- Want to outsell your competitors by 10 per cent?
- Want to grow your market share by 20 per cent?
- Want a 20 per cent market share gain?
- Have you got the bottle – to take our efficiency challenge? (This was the message in the milk bottle.)

– Want to increase productivity by 18 per cent?

– Interested in sales growth?

These examples are ideal for Tier 1 personalities. Remember, the message that you use for a CEO will be totally different to that for a production manager, say. This means, if you are well resourced, that you can have Campaign One with messages for CEOs, perhaps with a variety of messages to suit them. Campaign Two is for HR directors, and Campaign Three is for customer services managers because these are the three decision-relevant contacts that you target as a business. You can have as many campaigns as you do key prospect contacts or you can decide to focus your efforts and budget on just one level.

Notice also that all of the Benefit Questions above are closed. The purpose here is to engage the contact in a participative experience. Get them thinking or talking. Have an impact. If you get them to answer 'Yes' to a question ('Want to slash operational downtime by 14 per cent?') it seems likely that they might be moved to do something positive about it.

Each of the messages above would, of course, be followed by a call to action: 'Want to reduce your business costs by 12 per cent? Call Greg Anyon on 01321 125456.'

Of course, there's a whole range of other materials and activities out there that you can use, under a variety of headings. For ease I tend to put them all into the same blender and call them all 'promotional items' because that's how Cascade Selling categorizes them. Here is a sample list of a few:

– **Postcard** – pictures sell! Postcards are a lovely idea because they can fulfil so many of the key features required for a promotional item and are so versatile: they're inexpensive, and can carry high impact, high resolution graphics and a high impact message. They are also quick and easy to design and produce. In this environment there are few better ways of capturing attention and interest than a fantastic graphic which can literally stop anyone in their tracks. Think of the impact of the Benetton campaigns, for instance – you don't have to be as direct but pictures do grab attention and interest. Handwritten messages can work very well because they look personalized, while it is fine to have a printed address label. You can also take a few calculated risks with this medium. For example, the message might read: 'Hi Jim. Just thought I'd mention, an idea popped into my head while sipping Pina Coladas by the pool: we've been working with Peachy Corp. to help them dramatically improve their time to market. How interested are you in generating new product revenues faster? You can call me on 1234 567890 to discuss it!' A consultant that I worked with always sent postcards when on holiday to key prospects and customers and claimed great results!

– **Flyer** – focus on the benefits, not products. Use high impact graphics. Graphs and charts are good for Analyticals as more detailed information can be included.

– **Newsletter or Ezines** (electronic magazine) – these work quite well but resist the urge to just produce pulp: 'Bob in Accounts is a new dad' or 'New Radion 6000 breaks neutron threshold, again'. You've got to present key Buying Wins. You can also include evidence and testimonials of the gain that your prospect can enjoy.

– **Case study** – focus on high impact benefits or gains. Have a short version and a long version. The short version as an electronic (PDF) appetite-wetter and the long version printed. The Driver can see the proof and the Analytical can thoroughly research it.

– **CD business card** – spend a little money on a benefit-bashing media production and this item will really get the message across. Resist the temptation to half-cook this by spending too little on it – this is a new business **investment!**

– **Funky multimedia benefit presentation CDs** – this is the same as a business card but on CD which is more cost effective.

– **'How to' guides or articles** – do a little in-house electronic publishing. Self-help or business process enhancement guides are great PR and deliver a little speculative 'value'. Publish your expertise and share it a little. Get them to try it and they might like it.

– **Direct mail or letters** – don't bother unless they present a hard hitting Benefit Pitch. The longer the letter, the less likely a Driver is to read it. Your target-response for any letter that you design should be what Frostie said: 'About time one of you people got to the point! What are you selling?'

– **Events** – you can run a range of special events, with or without public speakers: conferences, exhibitions, high-end seminars, workshops, no-cost consultations and so on. Hire decent keynote speakers. They don't have to be famous, but make sure that they can communicate in the language of Tier 1s.

– **The ubiquitous website** – is your website a **big** Benefit Pitch or is it dull as dishwater? One of my clients is a large shipping company. They have advertising banners on the sides of huge buildings in prime locations like international airports. I can't give you exact dimensions but these things are **huge!** Maybe 100 metres x 50 metres. And one of the big attention-grabbing headlines that they use is: 'Save time!' This is a good start because it's a benefit and not a product. Now we're cooking. But think about the amount of Tier 1s that fly in and out of major airports every day. The banner is aircraft size – the Tier 1 **could not** miss it, even blindfolded! 'Save time' is as big a sales sin as 'Save money'. They've been so overclaimed by sales people over the years that no buying contact believes them any more. They're just too generic and watered down. Imagine that you've just been given a hanging space the size of a hockey pitch to scream your message out to a guaranteed high-level traffic of prospects! What would you say? Get this right and you're going to get enquiries from all the right people. How about:

'Want to reduce your business costs by 12 per cent?'

Or

'Want to boost productivity by 14 per cent overnight?' Followed by a big call to action 'Call Us on This Number...'

Think of your website as a HUGE banner. If you can cause Tier 1s to go on to your website (if that's part of your strategy) will it **immediately dazzle them with highly attractive Buying Wins** and make them want to contact you, or will it take away their will to live with boring product and service stuff? Combine the one second rule with the fact that Tier 1s have the attention span of a gnat and your home page better poke them in the eye with a sharp stick.

– If your website is not constructed like a lure, designed specifically to cause them to make contact, it is pointless.
– If your home page is just a mass of copy, it will fail.
– If it is product centric, it will fail.
– If it does not contain some high impact benefit messages, it will fail.

– If it is not easy to navigate, it will fail.

– If it does not give them repeated calls to action, it will fail.

– If it does not present them with some eye candy (graphics)…

In a Cascade Selling environment a website is not an on-line brochure. It also should NOT be owned by marketing, software jocks or internet creatives. It should be co-owned by them in conjunction with **sales**. After all – what is a website for if not to attract business? If getting the company website re-modelled is too big a mountain to climb, create a second site that is the portal for sales enquiries from Cascade activities. This site, of course, can be linked to the main one.

The categories of promotional item are not rigid. Some items have a higher cost than others. In order to create the right *blend* you have to have more than one item. The optimum, according to the best and the brightest, is 12 elements in the blend. If embarking on a Cascade Communications Campaign to a targeted major prospect, that's one per month if you have a year to burn, or if you are aiming at an accelerated penetration phase, perhaps one per week or per fortnight!

CAMPAIGNING

When used specifically for Cascade Communications, promotional materials lose their generic marketing characteristics and become a massively focused and powerful method of ramping up our ratios, and much more cost effectively than calling alone. If you are going to consider a campaign it should be matched against a database of frequent contact. First we send them an email, then next month a sachet of high quality hot chocolate, and the month after a mouse mat, followed the month after by a postcard and so on.

Of course, when physical contact is achieved, you take them off the campaign list **or** start campaigning other contacts that they suggest in their company!

Have you ever heard a customer say to you or their staff that they had to talk to you eventually because you were always banging on their door so persistently? Well, this is the same thing but it reduces the timespan involved and the level of effort.

EXAMPLE CASCADE COMMUNICATIONS PLAN

Item no.	Promotional item	Targeted at: Message:	On date:	Cost £
1.	Rubber duck	Jim Smith, Ops Mgr You'd be Quackers not to try our new Ops Synergy Survey	4/6/09	3 of 300
2.				
3.				
4.				
5.				
6.				
7.				
8.				
9.				
10.				
11.				
12.				
TOTAL COST				

Remember that with an email, letter or postcard you have a little more room for some *brief* but meaningful messages like who you have achieved a 12 per cent gain for and how (should you decide that this information would be beneficial). Everything, of course, will have your company name and logo on it, and a Call to Arms or Action: 'Call David Legg on +44 (0)1234 123456', etc. You never know, someone might even do it!

After the campaign begins, for each item sent the laws of probability suggest that the level of recognition and interest increases pro rata **if** you have got the message right.

NOW YOU'RE COOKING: LET'S HARNESS THE POWERHOUSE NETWORK

Heard of Linkedin? Of course you have: it's one of the many business network websites that have sprung up designed to get us acquainted with a lot of other business people. Sign up at www.linkedin.com and give it a try. It will connect you to some people who you don't know and reacquaint you with some that you haven't heard from in a while. Along the way you might do some business!

Cascade Selling focuses on gaining access to ivory towers where Guardians protect their Tier 1s rather effectively. But some organizations make our job much more difficult at a far earlier stage than contact. There are companies the world over who have a 'No Names' policy. This means that they will not hand out names on request. This has been around for a while and usually a search on the net can provide us with a contact. More difficult are the companies that will not release names, will not respond to emails, do not publish names on their website, and even in some cases broadcast that they will not talk to anyone who approaches them without invitation.

A small part of me goes into paralysis when I hear of this type of company.

I am literally stunned. These same organizations expect to find open doors when their sales people go out into the market, but are not interested in professional quid pro quo: they build fortresses to kill the selling approach of others. This is as potentially damaging to the transaction of business as price leadership is to company profits.

Thank goodness then for Linkedin and others like it. On the day that you are faced with the impenetrable faceless company with No Names, go online. As an example, go to the Linkedin home page, click on Advanced Search, and then put the company name into the relevant box and see what you get back! Even though you might not get the name of the specific contact that you want, other names are available whom you, or one of your colleagues, can approach.

BIG BANG

Wouldn't it be nicer though if we could get recommended to the business that we desire? Wouldn't life be easier if we could use the Name Dropper Pitch as our main Benefit Pitch?

One of my clients is a global player with operations in virtually every country in the world. They adopted the idea of creating an *internal* network that began in their Portuguese operation. The Portuguese published a list of their customers to the other countries in the group. In the event that they wanted to penetrate the customer operation in their own country, or wished to sell to a company in the supply or customer chain, they automatically had access to the names of valuable reference contacts. Each country then followed suit with a list of its own customers. As a result a contact and vertical marketing database was created in big bang time, at **no cost** and in an envronment where the information was closely controlled and monitored by the 'User Group'; in this case an international mix of sales people.

MY NETWORK

Send out an invitation to join your personal network! Send it to customers, colleagues, suppliers and anyone else that you ever heard of. You can invite them by email or verbally. Email is potentially less labour intensive but people are notoriously fickle at responding to what they classify as non-critical email. There are many ways of populating the network: **you do not have to publish customer lists** if you don't want to (for those of you who just went frothy at the idea). You can create a network of contacts for use on a case by case basis: 'We want to get into Krupp Steel – does anyone have any contacts we can use?' This is by far the safest method of using the network, but the old rule applies here: give a little and you get a lot. Trust your network – tell them who you work with – and they might surprise you by sharing much more.

Another good example of this comes from a training programme I was running for a major industrial supplier. It transpired during the course that one of the companies that these guys were targeting was a market leader 'Oops Up Side My Head' (made-up name). I know the marketing director of the target company and more importantly his PA. So I contacted the PA to ask if she could get me the name and direct dial number for a key contact that my training group were interested in. Not only did she do that, but she also facilitated an introduction!

GO BLIND ON NUMBERS

You've heard the saying: 'It's not what you know; it's who you know'? It goes without saying that a personal recommendation is worth its weight in gold and is the very foundation of the Name Dropper Benefit Pitch. The personal network is the business contact force multiplier: if you invite 20 people to join your network, and they each know 20 companies, that's a database of 400 companies. If they know three contacts per company, that's 1200 contacts. If they recommend the network to another 20 people each, you could go blind on the numbers. That's a **Powerhouse** network! And unlike a proprietary business network, people have joined your network with the stated purpose of operating as providers and recipients of prospect information.

Send out an email or pick up the telephone today and start your personal network. By Miller Time you'll be up to your neck in prospects! And every time you make a new and trusted contact, invite them into your network.

HARNESSING CASCADE SELLING TEAM ASSETS

Bringing non-sales people of whatever rank or commercial discipline into your Cascade Selling Team is not as easy as it sounds; it will never happen just because we invite them and definitely won't happen if we tell them to do it. In the companies where it happens well, I believe it does so because the sales people educate their colleagues to understand the need, opportunity and value of a prospect or customer. Or it happens because of a highly evolved organizational culture. The Tier 1 or Board promotes the practice of co-operation and team working, and actively takes part themselves.

DEM JOCKS: VALUABLE SALES ASSETS OR SALES PREVENTION OFFICERS?

A little while ago, on behalf of a client (a sales manager), I did a day of Field Sales Accompaniment with one of his sales people, selling portable IT hardware. The objectives of the day were not just to do some appointments but also to conduct some face-to-face cold calling aka prospecting aka door-knocking. Field Sales Accompaniment is often used to identify what skills a sales person has, and where they can stand some development. Frequently part of the objective behind the activity is to breathe a little enthusiasm and motivation into them and get them doing things that might be just outside their comfort zone.

We had two appointments scheduled for the day, and on both occasions we were joined by a product manager. A PM (I've also heard them called demonstration jockeys or dem jocks for short) in this client's organization is many things but one of their primary functions is to provide a technical demonstration service for sales people at the 'Present Proposition' stage of the sales Progression. Or that's what I thought they were for...

On our second appointment of the day I began to wonder. Cut to the chase: we arrived at 3.30 p.m. for a 4 p.m. initial appointment and took up residence in the car park. This was the first time we'd met the prospects, and it was one of those 'Show us your wares because we're *really* interested' kind of meetings – hardly ideal but plenty of promise. The spare half hour gave us time to meet with the PM, talk through our sales objectives and establish the PM's role in fulfilling them. The PM didn't arrive until 4.15 p.m. Ooh, spot the time pressure creeping in, not to mention the *impact* on the prospects of being late! We went in, made our apologies, and the PM started setting up his demonstration kit. While this was taking place, the sales person asked a range of questions to identify situation, need, decision process, and the impact of the needs (nice). He also asked what they wanted to see the product do (lovely). It was difficult not to get excited at the stream of buying signals that started flowing out. The two prospects kept drawing the PM into the conversation, giving him Key Purchase Criteria, and the PM kept nodding with an all-knowing smile on his face, but said nothing. He also didn't write anything down. I thought: 'Wow! Not only is this guy a technowiz, but he's also got total memory recall!'

So, the preamble out of the way and the kit set up, the PM began his product demonstration run. Now, it is worthy of note at this juncture that PMs are a fantastic asset. Their depth of product and application knowledge frequently goes way beyond that of a sales person and they invariably are capable of digging up additional needs that only expert knowledge can find. Add a sales person with finely tuned commercial skills and it's a marriage made in heaven, right? The sale is a dead certainty or a sure thing, yes?

The PM started talking about the broad and diverse capability of the product. Surprisingly, he was not working with the needs established and agreed by the sales person, but working instead from a mental check list and verbal demonstration of every feature in the box. He asked the odd question about suitability along the way. When one of the prospects said that a particular feature or capability was something they *didn't* need, the PM carried on presenting it regardless because, of course, they *might* need it at some unforeseeable point in the distant future. He paused after about 20 minutes to draw breath, and the glazed expression in the eyes of the prospects started to clear. During the course of these long 20 minutes the sales person had tried interjecting on a number of occasions to get the demo on course and to give it some desperately needed relevance, but to no avail. Thereafter, steam had started to escape from his ears. The key prospect said: 'Some of this is quite interesting, but about 60 per cent is going straight over my head.' The PM carried straight on like a rhino with the scent of tourist-filled Land Rover in its nostrils. At least he added in useful snippets of information like 'And because of the high levels of functionality of the kit you'll need to send your people on a training programme.' I thought the sales person was going to start frothing at the mouth.

At 5 p.m. the key prospect started looking at his watch – frequently. At 5.10 p.m. he said, 'Just to let you know guys but I need to leave this meeting at 5.15 p.m.' At 5.15 p.m. even though the sales person was trying to terminate the demonstration, and the prospects were walking from the meeting room back to their offices, the PM kept right on going. At 5.25 p.m. the key prospect said: 'Look; it's my wedding anniversary tonight and I'm taking my wife out to meet friends for dinner, and if I don't get out of here by 5.30 p.m.

on this one night of the year my wife is going to divorce me.' At 5.35 p.m. the sales person produced a crow bar out of nowhere and pried them apart, and by 5.45 p.m. we were back in our respective cars.

We didn't debrief with the PM in the car park, mainly because the sales person probably wouldn't have found it terribly easy to approach the conversation with any sense of positivity. I think at one point he was contemplating dining on the man's lungs. Part of his frustration, it became apparent, was based on the fact that this PM was notorious and had been spoken with on the subject of 'brevity and relevance' on numerous previous occasions. So, in rampant frustration the sales person said: 'So what the hell am I supposed to do?'

My reply was in two parts: (1) what is the probable outcome of the call? And (2) what can we do to prevent this in the future?

The call, although based on an early product demonstration (which is dangerous) held all the promise of an early sale. The net result was probably that we lost a very low cost of sale order for £5,000, and any future pull-through or recommendation business. It is highly likely that the prospects viewed the outcome as:

– Gosh, what a complicated product.
– Golly, isn't it difficult to use.
– And we'll have to take people out of the workplace for extensive training.
– Which will add both visible and hidden costs.
– And will they remember it all?
– And the product does so much more than we need.
– So we'll be buying a computer when all we actually need is a typewriter.
– I bet there's a product out there that is a much closer fit to our needs.
– I bet it costs less too.
– Shall we go see?
– And oh how we yawned!

Prevention *is* better than cure but I am far more inclined not just to prevent but also to empower, equip and motivate people to do things differently, and better. The answer to what we should do with one Dem Jock is the same as what we should do with all Dem Jocks! No: *you have to make them part of the process*. And we're not just talking about an individual function. This applies to all of the people that you need to involve when operating a selling team built to win major new business or strengthen your position in existing. You have to get them involved right from the start and help them to see just how critically important they are, and the best way to fulfil that importance. In this case, *technical* expertise is not enough in isolation, and flexing technical or intellectual muscle is dangerous. In the same way, sales expertise is not enough in isolation, without technical and marketing and production and so on.

THE PAYOFF

In pursuit of high value new business even the most talented Cascade sales people need support. You cannot afford to assume that any of the colleagues that you involve is equipped to help you achieve your sales objectives until they have proved it, or you have prepared them.

The technical resource, the product manager, in this true story serves quite nicely as a symbol for all of your company's resources. If you wish to harness assets and not be on the receiving end of liabilities all you need to do is master a few simple steps:

1. Sales and technical managers (or any kind for that matter) should foster strong mutual relations and promote them between their departments.
2. Each should speak publicly of the value of the other in our overall objective – satisfying specific customer needs profitably.

3. Invite each other to social jollies to breed team appreciation, working and relationships.

4. The sales person should brief the PM on call objectives, planning or structure, steps and stages, what the PM needs to do, and how the sales person will manage the call or the sale, well in advance.

5. Both should meet up in good time before the call to ensure that they discuss exactly what's going to happen, who is going to do it, how and when.

6. The sales person leads, and starts the meeting or demonstration by drawing out the situation, all of the Key Purchase Criteria, wants, needs, concerns, interests...

7. The PM then extrapolates any of these into additional needs based on their expert knowledge: 'If you suffer with lag on circuit X, do you also find that you get lock-up on circuit Y?'

8. The PM then presents specific benefits and features that satisfy those established and agreed needs.

9. The sales person keeps note throughout, putting ticks into each needs-box, and then summarizes this after the demo with the prospect, checking their agreement.

10. The sales person then moves the demonstration forward to the next stage in the sales process, whatever that may be.

11. Afterwards, the sales person and PM debrief to see what worked well and what can be improved on for the future. This could be in the car, or might even involve alcohol. In either case the sales person shows their appreciation.

'Mud against the wall' demonstrations or presentations are common enough; I don't doubt we have attended a few as members of the audience, or even been forced to make some ourselves. And some of them work from time to time. The presenter lays out their wares and a buying contact goes: 'Ooh, that looks interesting…' One in who-knows-how-many strikes a chord, and it's full speed ahead and never mind the icebergs.

When, however, we embark on a highly refined method for attracting and winning **big** new business, the company's lifeblood, there is no place for traditional product-based selling. We get much more for our effort, and a greater return on our investment, if we plan out some of the chance and build in a little certainty…

SUMMARY

THE FORTHCOMING NEGOTIATION

This book describes the Cascade Selling Process, not negotiation which is treated as a different but, of course, related subject. Disturbingly however I have seen Cascade sales people go all the way through the process, building value at every turn, only to see it all bleed away in the end-zone negotiation.

There is a genuine belief in the mind of buying negotiators that they will be able to negotiate every sales negotiator **down**. Many sales negotiators seem to believe that part of their job involves giving away their margins! I have witnessed this worrying mindset in more sales negotiators than I care to mention.

The good news is that the Cascade Process paves the way for highly productive negotiations.

Golden Sales Rule No. 749 says that at any and all costs we must resist having to sell to the purchasing department first. This is the kiss of death to the margins of many sales organizations and yet many sales people still pucker up for the big snog. Purchasing cares about bleeding our margins and getting the best deal for themselves and perceivably little else. Cascade sales people do not sell price and we do not wish to haemorrhage margins. As clichéd as it sounds we sell value – but not in the jargonized and meaningless sense of the word. The Cascade Strategy facilitates the creation of value from the first approach, made a million miles from purchasing. In cascading through the organization we create the image of a supplier that will invest itself in the customer. In producing a Payback spreadsheet we position ourselves as:

1. A supplier that conducts sufficient research to form a working knowledge of their business and the kind of challenges that they face.
2. We then work with them taking a problem-solving approach, identifying key issues in their business.
3. We provide bespoke solutions to those established and agreed needs.

4. We are seen not as an external supplier but as an essential internal asset in the smooth operation of their business, because we become their in-house efficiency consultants.

Not only are we sponsored by Tier 1 through the organization. We become sponsored by all the people to whom we did not *sell*, but worked with instead to identify problems, the cost of problems and then needs. In many cases this can negate the necessity for dealing with purchasing at all because this new supplier is deemed to be special, key or core.

However, even in the event that we have to deal with purchasing (which does happen) we end up dealing with them last and not first. Because we are the supplier of choice, it is not a question of lining up with two other transactional suppliers and the cheapest wins. The balance of power shifts, from purchasing (in the minds of many sales people) to the Cascade seller.

Picture this: the purchasing officer sits there in the end-zone negotiation, having kept you waiting for 45 minutes, shaking his head and 'tutting' as he allegedly reads your proposal (all of which are infamous negotiation tactics designed to unsettle you). Eventually he says: 'You'll have to do better than that' and the blood-letting fun begins!

With Cascade Selling, the balance of power is in *your* favour because purchasing has been told by Tier 1 et al.: 'This is the supplier – get the deal done.' Your response to 'You'll have to do better than that' is:

– 'Why?'
– 'If you want a cheaper price we're going to have to remove something. Which part do you want me to take out?'
– 'Our proposition is constructed like a Swiss watch – to deliver perfect results. Take out one component and it won't work. Which part do you want to take out?'

– 'Our proposal saves you £422k, and in nine days will pay for itself. It also puts £407k back onto the bottom line of the business. Forgive me but I don't understand – how do you expect us to discount this?'

Try not to swoon from the blood rushing to your head at this point. I know – the potential here is fantastic. After all those beatings that you've had to suffer over the years, to now be able in effect to say, 'Get stuffed!' is tantalizing, isn't it? But beware. Whilst it *is* possible at this point to win business without trading anything in the negotiation, I advise against it. A purchasing person who hasn't taken some flesh has not earned their keep, and will be your enemy for ever because you made them look incompetent and feel weak. They will work away in the background trying to bring you down. So give them something. Not discount, but something with a low cost to you and high value or market cost to them. Training (if you have trainers on the payroll) or consulting or similar. But don't just hand it over: trade it, *reluctantly*.

VODKA AND SLEEP DEPRIVATION

The problem is that 'Value' is a word that we all use every day and it has been so abused that certainly in the ears of buying contacts it means nothing. I'm not even sure they hear it! If as a Cascade sales person we're going to use it and then **prove** that we deliver it we'd better know what it means. This is a difficult one – I have asked hundreds of people for their definition of value and the answers range from as vague as a politician to as solid as a blancmange tennis racquet.

I was part of a sample group of 100 training professionals asked to define 'Value'. Ask a group of 100 'Experts' to define something and you should be good to go, right? Not so! We couldn't agree on the definition! So, in the true spirit of 'being an expert is: knowing when to call in the experts' we decided to call in scientists. If you're going to properly define something, you need someone who is good with equations – you need a mathematician. So we pulled together an Oxbridge team of seven scientists and mathematicians. Even now I am unable to confirm the split of participants from Oxford and Cambridge as it is still seen to be a highly contentious issue in some circles. So, we took seven boffins and just to make it interesting we decided to bring a real experimental feel to the event. We locked them in a sleep deprivation chamber for a week with nothing to eat or drink except vodka. At the end of the week we opened the door and they staggered into the light blinking – and babbling. Honestly, feed them on nothing but vodka, deprive them of sleep and they babble. Who would have thought? They babbled (two) equations (go figure).

The first equation is the complex version, and due largely I think to the amount of spirit that they consumed is incomplete:

$$V = PRB>PRC$$

What the equation says is that Value happens when the Perceived Relative Benefit is greater than the Perceived Relative Cost.

Or there's the simpler version:

$$V = B>C$$

This says that value happens when the benefit is greater than the cost. But this is still incomplete. We are missing the critical factor without which all of this is irrelevant:

$$V = (B>C)/Comp.$$

You will clearly be seen by your customer as the provider of tangible value when you can demonstrate to them that the benefits from your products and services far outweigh the cost. And it has to be better than your **competition** can provide. You have to offer them something different that has a beneficial value.

Regrettably the whole vodka scientist tale is a bit of fiction (obviously: Oxbridge scientists drink gin). The commonly recognized definition of value is not. In order to demonstrate that the benefits of your products and services far outweigh the costs, you have to be able to **show them**. You have to be able to **demonstrate it!** This is accomplished perfectly by the Payback spreadsheet. 'Better than your competition' goes some way towards the implication that innovation in the pursuit of competitive differentiation is a significant factor in acquiring new business. But anyone can design and produce a better product. Expecting that it will automatically open doors for them is the ruin of many a premature 'We're millionaires on paper' celebration. You can have the greatest product in the world but if the *right people* don't hear about it *in the right way* it'll end up in the creative graveyard with thousands of others. The traditional dumping of feature functionality does not make major sales...

The Cascade Selling of benefits does!

CONCLUSION

I went into sales 25 years ago at the tender age of 18. If asked, I would sheepishly confess to you that I entered the profession because I wanted to drive a nice car that someone else paid for, wear a suit and not get my hands dirty. Very quickly, though, I discovered that there is much more to a job in sales than mere symbols.

This is the greatest profession in the world. Back then it was one of the few with virtually zero entry-level requirements. With not much more than some spirit, reasonable communication skills and a bit of self-belief or personal resilience you could get a job in sales and potentially flourish. The surprising thing is that 25 years on, little has changed. In sales, unlike so many other professions, if you have the desire you can truly be master of your own destiny, dictating not just how much you earn but also how you earn it. You don't have to be chained to a desk or confined to an office – you can be out there in the world making hay while the sun shines. All you have to do to be highly successful is to identify the important things to get right, and then keep getting them right!

So for the first few years of being a sales guy I charged around the place with boundless energy and enthusiasm, kicking down doors and presenting persuasive arguments. I developed some skills, found my level and got on with it. And I could have continued in that way for the rest of my life and enjoyed a reasonable level of success. But one day, I lost a deal. I was used to working the percentages – so you win some and you lose some: but this one was significant, and losing it *hurt*. Not just my revenues, or achievement against target, but also my pride. So I asked the 64,000 dollar question: 'Why? Why did I lose that deal?' You don't get many threshold moments in a sales career, but this was mine. To this point I had been anything but analytical. I had charged in with all guns blazing, winning business and growing accounts through little more probably than the power of personality.

Now I wanted to know why sales fail, and for the first time I began to question the causal factors in selling. What makes a sale fly, and what makes it die?

As a sales leader and then a training consultant I have spent hundreds of hours listening to and observing sales people in live selling situations. It's amazing what you can observe when you shut up and listen and as a result have helped thousands of sellers and others to refine their sales approach and be infinitely more productive.

As a sales person do you ever feel like you're stuck in a rut? Like you need to be doing something different or better? Do you ever feel like you're only getting a small percentage of the sales that you approach, and are missing out on a big slice of the cake? Do you want to sell more? Then you have to be analytical about selling and buying. You have to think about and develop process, skills and techniques. **And** you have to tune in to the human factor: behaviour, emotions, logic, causal factors, attitudes, motivations and so on.

Do all that, and you can still crash and burn! The critical catalyst is that you then have to go and do something about it. You have to identify what you could be doing better and then you have to go and try it – experiment! It doesn't matter if it works first time or not. It matters that you identify the opportunities and plan to fulfil them. And when it doesn't quite work – improvise, adapt and overcome until you get it right.

It is possible to stand still in selling. It is possible for talent to remain undiscovered. It is possible not to progress and to become stagnant. And often, much of this can happen without the victim even knowing about it. If you're reading this it will be because you read the book. Fantastic! Now all you have to do is take the material from the book that you thought worked for you and apply it in your **daily** sales activities. Apply it and modify it until it works, and then build it into your personal style. But don't stop there – then go out and buy another book, and another. Don't restrict yourself to sales. As a sales person your knowledge is a direct contributor to your credibility, success and progression. So get well versed in negotiation, key account management, marketing, business finance, presentation skills, motivation, people management and so on.

There is only one person who is genuinely interested in your development and success, and that's you. Who's going to do it if you don't? If you embark on this course of analytical self-development, I wish you the very best of luck – which in truth you won't need. And if you are in need of a little inspiration or a few ideas from time to time you can always visit my website www.redsector.co.uk

I leave you with this thought. A few years ago, on hearing news of a promotion that I had received, a colleague sent me a congratulations card. The message for me summed up everything in the selling profession:

'Good things come to those who wait... Great things come to those who go out and get them!'

ABOUT THE AUTHOR

GREG ANYON is a UK-based sales consultant, coach and trainer, who works with companies and sales people to literally help them *sell more*. His Cascade Selling method has been tested and proven with delegates across Europe, the United States and Asia in small, medium and very large companies. He specializes in sales, performance sales management, negotiation, presentation, and key accounts, and heads a UK-based sales training consultancy (www.redsector.co.uk).